FORGIVE
ME NOT

A FAMILY MEMOIR OF REGRETS
AND SECOND CHANCES

CATHERINE RAPHEL STEWART

Archway Publishing books may be ordered through booksellers or by contacting:

Archway Publishing
1663 Liberty Drive
Bloomington, IN 47403
www.archwaypublishing.com
844-669-3957

ISBN: 978-1-6657-1388-7 (sc)
ISBN: 978-1-6657-1386-3 (hc)
ISBN: 978-1-6657-1387-0 (e)

Library of Congress Control Number: 2021921022

Print information available on the last page.

Archway Publishing rev. date: 11/02/2021

CONTENTS

Le bonheur est salutaire pour le corps, mais c'est le chagrin qui développe les forces de l'esprit. (Happiness is beneficial for the body, but it is grief that develops the powers of the mind)

Marcelle Proust – *À la Recherche du Temps Perdu (In Search of Lost Time)*

This book is dedicated to my parents
Claudine and Gabe Raphel

In the summer of 1994 my husband David and I were living in Tranquility, a small hamlet in Sussex County, New Jersey, painstakingly rehabbing a stone farm house built in 1732. We decided to take a break from this project by joining my parents in France at my aunt Poussy's castle in Provence. She had married a count, which by default made her a countess, and she was doing her own meticulous rehabbing of an old structure. We thought we could get some tips from her.

The kind of rehabbing she was undertaking was well beyond our budget but the trip was certainly not wasted. Not only did we spend several enjoyable days in a castle with entertaining family members, but a conversation took place that got me focused on my heritage. One night after dinner the men went to play billiard and sip cognac. The women—Poussy, my mother and me—went to the living room where my aunt played an opera record, translating each word from Latin to French; complete with intense emotion. The next morning, Dad, David and I were at the breakfast table and I said to my husband:

"I don't want you to think all French families are like this." I meant the castle and its trappings.

Without hesitation, Dad contributed:

"Yes, they're not all this dysfunctional."

That's when it first occurred to me that I had an unusual family and a story worth telling. When we got home from France, I asked my parents to send me information about their families and their early years. I especially wanted to know why my father became a third generation perfumer and how he ended up practicing his craft in America.

This launched me into writing this book. Initially, the research stayed in folders that were moved from New Jersey to Kentucky, California, Virginia and finally to Beaufort, South Carolina in 2011. It took another nine years and a global pandemic to inspire me to finally write *Forgive Me Not*.

CHAPTER 1

JULIETTE-ANTOINETTE, FEBRUARY 2, 1956

GABE

This day I knew would stay with me forever. When I woke up and looked out the window, I was shocked to see it had snowed overnight! This was very unusual in my home town of Golfe-Juan, a small Mediterranean village in the heart of the French Riviera where I had lived most of my life. The only other time it had snowed was in 1929 when I was nine years old.

I had planned out this day for months and yet I was dreading what lay ahead of me. When I finally got on the road in a borrowed car, I passed all the familiar shops—from our boulangerie (baker), to our boucher (butcher), and finally our épicier (grocer). I wondered if I would ever see these merchants again. Within minutes, I was traveling very slowly up the familiar hill. I parked in front of the house and thought: this is probably the last time I will ever go into this house. As I got out of the car, the cold air made me gasp. I was careful to avoid slipping on the snow.

I walked up to the gate of Juliette-Antoinette, the house named after my mother. Her grandparents had built it, and I had been born there. It was not a large, majestic house like Sainte Marie-à-Py, the former family home where I had lived most of my youth, but it was a beauty in its own way. Surrounded by a tall metal fence mostly covered by a variety of vines, the several-story stone house had the familiar quarry tile roof. There were three levels of gardens, including an orchard in the lower back where I had grown grapes for homemade wine. Best of all, when you stood on one of the bedroom balconies, you had a clear view of the Mediterranean below. I loved this house.

Suddenly, I felt such despair I could hardly breathe. So many people had depended on me, and I had let them down. I had been fiercely proud of my success, but now I had nothing left—and all of it was my fault.

I opened the house gate, and its familiar creaking sound made me smile but also made me sad. Walking slowly on the snow-covered stone walk, I made my way toward the house. As I looked around at the landscaped garden that held many shrubs and exotic plants, I shook my head in disbelief at the snow that covered the grounds. I walked up the stone steps onto the terrace, and for a moment I was transported to happier times when family and friends gathered for delicious French dinners. I could almost hear the lively conversation among the opinionated French men and women and taste the delicious food the maid Madeleine would have prepared. Today the patio furniture was gone and the snow hid much of the stone surface. I stepped carefully around to the left side of the house and unlocked the door.

Juliette-Antoinette was much more than a beautiful home that held so many wonderful memories. It meant everything that was important to me—family, tradition, and especially success. I knew the house well since my family had moved back in when I was in my twenties. My father, a gentle man with little business sense, had lost a great deal of money in the stock market. Eventually the family was forced to sell various parcels of prime

French Riviera land in order to support themselves. When all the land was gone, they sold Sainte Marie-à-Pie, the big house on the hill, and moved into Juliette-Antoinette, the smaller one.

On this snowy February day, I had come to Juliette-Antoinette to collect several pieces of luggage containing clothes and other personal belongings my wife Claudine and I were taking to America. A third generation French perfumer, I was now without a job; soon I would be without a country to call home.

Before going any further into the house, I sat on the bench in the foyer next to the kitchen. This was going to be much harder than I imagined. I was not prepared for the emotions that took hold of me. I had not planned this into the day.

"Growing up in a wealthy family can be a curse," I often told friends in my latter years. "You adopt an exaggerated sense of entitlement and you assume nothing can ever be taken from you."

I was wrong about that, and as I sat in the foyer of my beloved family home that fact was made clear. I got up from the bench and went into the living room. Even today this room took my breath away. I had christened it the Napoleon room—and it was most appropriately named. The walls were covered from floor to ceiling with a rich, hunter-green silk cloth imported from China, and the detailed woodwork was left natural.

The period Empire furniture included a massive wood and glass bookcase containing a priceless collection of miniature tin soldiers representing Napoleon's army. The Emperor was my idol, and as I had done many times before, I opened the bookcase, picked up some of my favorite soldiers, and moved them around. I had read every book I could find about Napoleon and had selected each tin soldier based on that research. I could even tell you the town or shop where I had purchased each piece.

I was also the proud owner of an extremely rare picture book about Napoleon. Only five copies of the book existed, and the other four were in museums. Ironically, Napoleon had landed in Golfe-Juan in March 1815 with 600 men when he escaped from exile on the island of Elba. From there he returned to Paris during a 100-day campaign that ultimately led to his defeat at Waterloo.

"This room says success," I used to say with arrogance. "It's a room fit for an emperor and perfect for us."

As I walked around the living room that day, I acted like a sponge and soaked up every detail since this could be my last time here. I also recalled the party Claudine and I gave to celebrate the new Juliette-Antoinette when the renovations were completed. It had been a fabulous evening with more than 100 young people dancing late into the night. Our daughters were vacationing in Italy that summer with our Nanny, but they heard all about the party when we came to visit them the following weekend. We brought them a caramelized sugar replica of the house which had been perched on top of a two-foot-high cake.

Those were the days I thought would last forever; I was young, arrogant, and only cared about making money and having fun. The future was something I rarely thought about, because I assumed it was secure.

I walked out into the main foyer and climbed the expansive, curved, marble staircase to the second floor. There once had been a very large birdcage next to the staircase, displaying a collection of exotic birds. They were my wife's joy, and she had named each of these birds after royalty. She spent hours caring for them to make sure they thrived. Today, only the birdcage remained. All the birds had died suddenly when our former life had ended two years ago. From that day on, she was convinced birds were a bad omen.

The suitcases I came to retrieve were in the bedroom where Claudine had left them several days earlier. While I was spending my last few minutes in the house, she was with our daughters at her aunt and uncle's house getting them settled. She was also trying to explain why they could not go with us to America.

I grabbed the bags and was about to go downstairs when I stopped, put the bags down, and walked into the bedroom our daughters had shared. Since the twin beds and matching dresser were gone, the room felt cold and stark where once it had been filled with joy. I walked to the French doors, opened them, and stepped out onto the balcony. Displayed below was an unobstructed view of the sky-blue Mediterranean, the Côte D'Azur personified. It took my breath away and made me cry—something I did rarely.

I had to leave before the heartbreak became too much to handle. I grabbed the bags, went back down the stairs, and was almost out the door when I noticed a frame on the foyer wall. It was my prized Rudyard Kipling poem "If" translated in French—a version I always thought was much better than its original English.

> *Si tu peux voir détruit l'ouvrage de ta vie* (If you can see your life's work destroyed)
>
> *Et sans dire un seul mot te mettre à rebàtir* (And without saying a word begin to rebuild)
>
> *Ou perdre en un seul coup le gain de cent parties* (Or lose in just one move the gain of 100 hands)
>
> *Sans un geste et sans un soupir* (Without a gesture or a sigh)
>
> Both versions go through a litany of human challenges, which can be conquered or overlooked, and they end with:
>
> *Et ce qui vaut bien mieux que les rois et la gloire* (And what is better than kings and glory)
>
> *Tu seras un homme, mon fils* (You will be a man, my son)

More than ever before, the poem spoke to me that day. I grabbed the frame and put it into one of the suitcases. I knew Claudine would understand why I had to take it with us.

I was so anxious to leave the painful memories behind that I forgot about the snow on the patio. When I heard my mother calling me from across the street, I hurried to get to her. Suddenly I slipped on the wet surface. I dropped the heavy bags and tried to break my fall with my left arm. As I hit the ground an excruciating pain shot from my shoulder, and I knew immediately I was badly hurt. Leaving the bags where they had scattered, I grabbed my left arm and walked slowly toward the gate and out into the street.

The pain was almost unbearable. I slowly crossed the street and climbed the exterior staircase to my mother's apartment. When she saw me come through the door she knew something was very wrong. My mother, although devastated that I was leaving for America, quickly put aside her sorrow to contact a doctor.

The doctor arrived shortly and told me my shoulder was dislocated; I had to go to the hospital. When he learned Claudine and I were scheduled to begin a ten-day ocean voyage to America that night, he strongly advised me to cancel our plans. I was too proud to admit to my long-time family doctor that we had to leave that night; we had spent much of our remaining money on two non-refundable one-way tickets.

At the hospital, I was so badly anesthetized I told the doctor when my shoulder came back to its rightful place. Needless to say, I suffered.

I couldn't help but wonder if my dislocated shoulder was an omen—one more thing that went wrong. I wondered if the decision to go to America was a mistake.

That decision had not been easy for us, but it was the only one possible—we were out of options. We would be saying goodbye to a country we had loved that now did not love us back. We would board the ship that snowy day in February as poor immigrants seeking a better life, leaving behind sailing on a friend's yacht, exciting weekends in Paris, and expensive restaurants. Most heartbreaking, we would leave our two young daughters behind. Claudine, who had attended the best finishing school in Paris, had no other formal education and could not speak English. I would refuse pain medication for my throbbing shoulder and leave France with my arm in a sling and my pride left on the pier in Cannes.

CHAPTER 2

MY FUTURE SECURED

GABE

Frankly, I was surprised but pleased when Catherine asked me about my family background and how I became a third generation perfumer. Of my four children, she would have been the last one I would have thought would care, but that's another story for later.

We all have interesting family stories, some of which we can't repeat. Many of us also have strange family members, some of whom we don't acknowledge. My family included its share of characters but for the most part they were pretty boring – that is, until I was born. But to trace the start of my perfumer's career, I first have to go back to my parents' families.

My mother's people were Italians who migrated to France in the early 1800s and became one of the oldest and wealthiest families in Vallauris, a small town just three miles up the hill from Golfe-Juan on the French Riviera. Initially this sleepy little town was known mostly for its pottery and ceramics, as well as its large population of communists, but it later gained notoriety when the artist Picasso lived there from 1948 to 1955.

My mother Juliette was the only child of Pierre Jourdan and his wife Euphrasine Gallou. As was the custom then, my grandfather added his wife's surname to his and so he became Pierre Jourdan-Gallou. This custom seemed a bit weird but also very upper class; almost like royalty. So that pleased me.

My grandfather Pierre was a well known philanthropist in Vallauris who gave away a lot of money during his lifetime. Fortunately, he earned a lot more than he gave away. That made him unique among the rest of the men in my family. When my grandparents died in May 1929 within days of each other at ages 70 and 69, the whole town attended their funerals in recognition of the many charities they had initiated or supported. My mother often talked about their generosity when I was a child, trying to instill in me the value of giving back to those less fortunate.

On my father's side, there is little reliable documentation as to his family's genealogy. My father Narcisse also had parents with double last names—Raphel-Carbonel—and they had three children. Years ago I found an old piece of paper among my father's documents; it was from a heraldist, someone who researches ancestries. The paper stated: "This letter claims the name of a Raphel ancestor appears on a list of people from 'distinguished families' who were knighted by King Louis XIV in 1696." Although many of my family members clung to this bit of fame, anything to make them less boring, this factoid is most likely total bullshit.

Both of my grandfathers were self-made men. My maternal grandfather Jourdan-Gallou built pottery manufacturing plants in the south of France and also managed a large coal operation. My paternal grandfather Raphel-Carbonel was the first in our family in the perfume business. Sadly he died of a heart attack at 49 and the perfume business was taken over by relatives who lacked both his business sense and his work ethic. By the time my father joined the business, it was already in a weakened state. Unfortunately this propensity for poor management would be repeated in future generations.

Although I was never told why my grandfather got into the

perfume business, there is no doubt two factors played a major role: his nose and where he lived.

First, anyone going into this business must have a nose (le nez in French) for scents. I don't know how he discovered he had this talent, but he passed it on to my father who then passed it on to me. That is how I ultimately became a third generation French perfumer. I'm happy to report two of my four children were blessed with the right nose, and they went into the business.

Initially I did not want to become a perfumer. The family business was not doing well when I got out of college and my father recommended that I choose another career. But perfumery was a natural for me. When I was in my teens, my father tested my nose and declared I had the gift. This should impress you since there are more than 2,000 different perfume scents, each with multiple ingredients. I had to know not only every ingredient in each scent, but the specific percentage of each.

Second, my grandfather lived in Vallauris which was just 25 miles southeast of Grasse, where the perfume industry started back in the 18th century. In fact, Grasse is still today considered the perfume center of France and the perfume capital of the world.

If you do any research on the perfume industry, you will find that it did not begin in France, although many people think it did. It actually goes back as far as ancient Mesopotamia, Egypt and maybe China. During the Renaissance, Catherine De' Medici, wife of King Henry II, is credited with introducing perfumes in Europe.

So how did a small town like Grasse end up as the perfume capital of the world? Well it can be traced back to the 12th century when Provence and the Côte D'Azur had a large tanning industry which gave off many bad odors. It took four more centuries however before something was done about it—and that was when perfumes were first used to mask the tanning stench. Also the climate in that part of France is particularly well suited to growing the plants used to make fragrances, such as jasmine, lavender, rose, mimosa and orange blossom.

It wasn't just the climate that drove the industry's growth; it was also being able to attract people with a refined sense of smell, and the same kind of perfume "artists" still work in Grasse today. At last count there were only 50 of these noses working there and getting paid handsomely for their unique talent.

In addition to the perfume trade, Grasse is also known today for attracting actors and writers, as well as for being the city in which the famous French singer Edith Piaf died. In fact her most famous song "La Vie en Rose" might have been inspired by the town's aroma.

When I was old enough to understand the intricacies of my father's and grandfather's profession, I also learned the perfume business was a recession-proof industry.

"No matter the health of the economy, people still spend money on scents" my predecessors often told me.

I'm not just talking about fine fragrances that people spray on themselves. The perfume business includes all products that have a scent. Since this represents a huge number of consumer goods, the industry is extremely lucrative for those lucky enough to have the gift for its creation, production and marketing.

Not only was I lucky to inherit the necessary "nose" to enter a recession-proof industry, but I also landed in an affluent family. When my mother Juliette and father Narcisse were married at 20 and 21 respectively, they united the two wealthiest families in Vallauris. There were so many guests at the wedding they had 24 horse-drawn carriages to take them to the church and then to the reception. I still have a very large framed photograph of the newlyweds dressed in their finest clothes and looking much older than their young ages. I have begged my children to make sure that once I'm gone this photograph doesn't end up in an estate sale and then in some cheesy diner just to cover a blemished wall. My parents certainly deserve better than that.

As soon as they were married, my parents quickly focused on starting a family and in 1910 my sister Marcelle was born, followed by my brother Claude in 1912. My parents had just five years together before my father was drafted into the army at the beginning of World War I, where surprisingly he turned down officers' school and served as a sergeant. As a result, he saw a lot of action and was wounded twice; the second wound occurred in a village called Sainte Marie-à-Py, which later became the name of one of his houses. My father earned the Croix de Guerre with two stars and the Medaille Militaire, which is the highest military decoration in France. He was the last Raphel to earn such military honors. In addition to the wounds he sustained, his health was also greatly compromised by mustard gas. He came home a different man.

Precisely nine months after my father returned from the war, I was born in Juliette-Antoinette on December 9, 1919. I was named Gabriel Bernard; the first name in honor of my uncle who also became my godfather. A year later, we moved to Sainte Marie-à-Py, the big house diagonally across the street.

When my father finished college after the war, he joined his father's perfume company in charge of production and spent the rest of his life in that business. It was never profitable but my father never thought about changing course. By the time he died in 1949, the company was in very bad financial condition and Sainte Marie-à-Py had to be sold to pay off debts incurred from law suits against the business. To give you an indication of the kind of property we are talking about, today a multi-story condominium complex occupies the spot once held by the house.

I revered my parents and grandparents, as did many people who knew them. My father was a very mild and quiet man with an unfortunate knack for losing a great deal of money in the stock market, aided by several shifty advisors. Because my father had to shoulder a series of lawsuits after his father's death, he eventually had to sell his father-in-law's pottery plants in addition to the family home in order to pay off those debts.

My father died in 1949 when he was just 64 years old.

My mother Juliette lived to 79 and from the day my father died she only wore black clothes. She always carried a rosary and moved the beads through her fingers as she prayed. She had always been the domineering figure in the marriage; very strong and even more so religious. At Christmas time she displayed a very elaborate nativity scene in the living room, featuring people and animal model figures, and each day she moved the figures a few inches toward the baby in the manger just as it would have taken place at Jesus' birth. Most of her conversations focused on Jesus, Mary and God. Sometimes she added the Holy Ghost.

Because my father's health had been so compromised by the war, my mother bore all responsibility for child rearing, which included managing my brother Claude who was mentally challenged as well my sister Marcelle who was at best emotionally fragile. While I was neither struggling mentally nor emotionally, I was nevertheless the most difficult one to reign in. From an early age, I adopted a keen interest in living big and having fun. Although I loved and respected my parents, I was determined to explore my own interests and passion. In spite of being far more challenging to contain than my siblings, I was my mother's favorite and she doted on me well into my adulthood.

This did not sit well with my sister. The more Marcelle tried to compete with our mother's attention, the more I rose to the occasion and earned more praise. I never had any problems with my brother Claude; he was simply too challenged to be a problem. Marcelle, on the other hand, was devious and angry at the same time.

Once when I was in church with my mother, which happened quite regularly, Marcelle went up to the confession booth and came out again very quickly. Since I was old enough to know what you're supposed to do in confession I asked my mother why Marcelle got out of there so fast.

"She has absolutely no sins to confess, my child" said my very pious mother. And this floored me in light of what I knew about Marcelle and her calculating character. Even at a young age, I determined she must have lied in the confessional.

By the time I was a teenager Marcelle had found a husband and moved out of the house so she stopped torturing me. Unfortunately, the chap did not last long because he quickly realized the family had already gone through much of their wealth. And when their child was still-born, he left her the very next month. So we ended up having Marcelle move back in the house and she quickly took up her campaign of hate against me.

As to my brother Claude, he was so intellectually challenged that he could never function on his own. As a consequence he never left home, never held a job and lived out his later life with Marcelle. I felt very sorry for him as he was a very sweet man but other than giving him money there was little else I could do.

Frankly, the only thing I had in common with my siblings was our last name. As I got older, I realized life was a lot more fun beyond the walls of my family's home. By the time I was fourteen, I spent less and less time at home and more time playing poker and chasing pretty girls in the village.

My parents had no interest in social activities, so they discouraged me from wasting hours on what my father referred to as "the frivolous pastimes of the young." To obey them, but still meet my needs, every night I kissed my parents goodnight and went to my room until the rest of the household was asleep. I then quietly went out the door and ran to the village where I partied all night, often winning at poker and charming the local girls. I always managed to get home before anyone woke up. This schedule worked very well for me then but would plague me with insomnia when I got older.

Since Golfe-Juan was a very small village and my nightlong

escapades were rather frequent, I soon had chased and caught the best of the local young ladies. That's when I decided to expand my horizons beyond Golfe-Juan to experience life more fully. In 1937 I left home to study law and literature in Aix en Provence. I had no idea what I would do with either of these disciplines since I had no intention of becoming an attorney nor was I cut out to teach. I was, however, thoroughly enjoying life in Aix—spending my days in restaurants playing poker and chasing young women at night.

Since school was always easy for me I spent little time studying. I was smart enough to get mostly As; except for math. I never passed a single math course but since I excelled in all other subjects, my professors kept moving me to the next grade. They accepted that I was incapable of learning math. My failure in this subject would end up costing me dearly later on.

It was during those years of carefree, narcissistic existence in Aix en Provence that I fine tuned my sense of humor, without erasing the provincial nature I earned in Golfe-Juan. Most importantly, I decided I would succeed at whatever I chose to do. After all, I had looks, brains, charisma and very good family connections.

I stayed in Aix en Provence until 1939 and then went back home to Golfe-Juan in the spring. There was so much uncertainty and fear in Europe over Hitler's aggression that I thought it was best for me to be home. In the fall, France declared war on Germany when the Nazis invaded Poland. Since I was still undecided about a career path, I decided to bide my time working in the perfume business with my father. I considered this just a stopgap position until something better would surely come along after the war was over, which most people thought would be a short time.

So 1939 was an important year for me. Not only did I experience France's entry into World War II and the beginning of my perfumer's career, but a third memorable event took place in June. That's when I met a gorgeous tiny French girl who stole my heart and kept it for the rest of my life. She'll have to tell you that story, as she tells it better than I do.

Although the war was anything but short, I was lucky to spend all of it in Golfe-Juan. Yes we all hated the Nazis and suffered with rations and having to live among people who had invaded our country. I had a job, I lived in a nice house and no one in our family or among our friends lost their lives. Since there weren't that many German soldiers on the French Riviera, our lives were not as impacted as those who lived in the northern parts of France.

Although I was never in the French army, I ended up serving in the US Army for three months through an interesting set of circumstances. In June of 1944, the Allied Forces landed in Normandy and began liberating France. During World War II, there were no organized resistance efforts on the French Riviera, so any defiance toward the Nazis happened on an individual basis. This is how I had one chance to make a difference. On August 15, 1944, <u>Colonel Bill Yarborough's</u> paratroopers jumped down into Le Muy, a village in Provence. They advanced rapidly but were stopped at Mandelieu, a suburb of Cannes, by the heavily-armed German infantry. When I learned about this, I was very frustrated because liberation seemed so close and yet was taking too long.

I could see German troops evacuating until very few of them were left. However, the Americans did not know that the Germans had left behind a powerful screen of troops armed with bazooka-like weapons called Panzerfaust, an anti-tank weapon they used against the enemy with devastating effects. Somehow I had to warn the Allies about this.

On that August day, I got on my small motorbike and rode to Mandeleiu. Leaving the bike in a ditch, I walked west and suddenly found myself looking straight at an American paratrooper. I told him the Germans had practically evacuated well beyond

Cannes but had left behind a small but dangerous platoon. The paratrooper did not believe their forces were reduced since a serious battle the previous night had claimed American injuries. Evidently I was persuasive enough so the paratrooper took me to meet his commanding officer—Colonel William Yarborough, a man who was to figure prominently in my future.

Colonel Yarborough took me into his unit, where I served from August to November of 1944. The unit immediately started moving toward Cannes and liberated the city that evening. The next day they pushed on toward Golfe-Juan and that night Colonel Yarborough and two of his officers slept at Sainte-Marie-à-Py. It was during my brief stint in the US Army that Colonel Yarborough suggested jokingly that I should consider immigrating to the US someday.

CHAPTER 3

MY TURBULENT CHILDHOOD

CLAUDINE

I was also surprised Catherine wanted to know about my family. Our second daughter was the rebellious one, adopting a challenging attitude in her teens and charming us with it for more than ten years. During that time she was against everything we represented -- our lifestyle, values and beliefs. So naturally, I was stunned she was interested in my early life and family background.

In any case, somewhat like Gabe's my background also included a pretty amazing lifestyle. However, unlike Gabe who only knew wealth, I spent my first fifteen years on a rollercoaster ride of uncertainty. Sometimes we had incredible wealth. At other times we didn't have money for food. This was because my father Roger Capgras was a consummate wheeler and dealer with absolutely no scruples. A master of deceit, he practiced on everyone he knew—including his own family.

Catherine once asked me what attracted Gabe and me to each other. It simply was a matter of total opposites. He was entertained by my dysfunctional family while I was attracted to the normalcy of his.

Unlike the Raphels, my parents came from very modest

backgrounds—they worked hard but rarely got ahead. My red-headed mother and her sister Charlotte and her sister Suzanne, or Zaza as she was called, broke that mold. They wanted a better life and both married entrepreneurs who chose interesting occupations and, eventually, earned a lot of money.

My parents Roger Capgras and Charlotte Barras were born in 1900. Roger was an only child, most likely because his parents Rachel and Antonin hated each other most of their lives, or so I've been told. They were both teachers and only managed to stay together a few years. I am convinced their son was permanently scarred by his parents' destructive relationship.

My father must have had a horrible childhood. He mostly lived with his mother who constantly bad mouthed his father. The few times the couple was together they accused each other of terrible things in front of their son. I suspect one or both of my grandparents physically abused my father.

My grandmother Rachel was mean and quite smelly. We called her the mean Grandma. My grandfather Antonin was no better catch—he was as arduous a politician, serving as mayor of a small town on the Atlantic coast, as he was a philanderer. At one time he lived with two sisters and their mother, and all three women were his mistresses at the same time! Antonin and Rachel died a few months apart when they were 85. I learned these sordid details from my mother, and they helped to explain my father's numerous character flaws.

My parents met in school and were married in September 1921. Charlotte's sister Zaza was her maid of honor but when she refused to partner with Roger's diminutive friend, my father asked his taller boss Charles Neveux to escort Zaza instead. This turned out quite well because Zaza and Charles were married six months later and stayed together more than 50 years— building a successful business as well. Since they lived near us most of their lives, they figure prominently in my upbringing and I always considered them a second set of parents. Fortunately, they were far more normal than my own parents.

From my recollection, I can tell you there was nothing in my father's behavior during the early years of my parents' marriage that could have warned my mother about his future actions.

My mother Charlotte had three children—my brother Pierre, then me two years later, and 14 years after that my younger sister Francine, (forever known as "Poussy" which loosely means little chicken in French). Zaza could never have children so she dotted on her nieces and nephew all of her life.

My father had a master's degree and went into business rather than follow his parents into teaching. He started a broom factory with Charles Neveux, selling each broom at a loss. This was followed by another business venture with Charles in the Loire Valley, but that too failed. Both times Roger's parents had to bail them out financially.

The two couples then rented a house together in a Paris suburb where they shared one mattress and one box spring; each couple taking turns sleeping on one or the other. This is where I was born in September 1924.

My mother told me the only people present at my birth were a half-drunk midwife and my aunt Zaza. I sure hope my mother ended up on the mattress that day.

Since Zaza did not have a car, she put my two year old brother Pierre in a wheelbarrow and went out to find my father to tell him he now had a daughter. She went to his place of business and learned he had been fired months before. Poor Zaza was so afraid to tell her sister this news that she chose to stay away all day, carting Pierre around in the wheelbarrow on the streets of Paris.

So barely three years into the marriage, my father was lying about where he worked. Soon my mother also suspected he was lying about who he was spending time with. At this stage of their marriage, they argued about many things.

For example, my brother and I ended up with strange name combinations because my parents also argued about my brother's name. My mother wanted to call him Pierre but my father insisted on the name Claude. A compromise was reached with Claude Pierre but since my brother always hated the name Claude and our father was rarely around, we always called him Pierre.

Since my father was not there when I was born, it only seemed natural my mother would get to pick my name and she decided I would be Claudine and Pierette would be my middle name.

A month after I was born, the two couples moved to Paris for jobs. This time they got separate apartments and each had their own mattress and box springs. Clearly, things were looking up.

My father was smart and very persuasive, and little by little our life improved. We moved to a better apartment in the Montmartre section of Paris and even had a maid. Up to that point in our childhood, my father had been very kind to his children and even often played with us. He was also very nice and attentive to our mother. But that would not last long.

I should tell you that I was always my father's favorite and this really made my brother very jealous. Pierre was very protective of our mother. When he was very young, he learned our father was spending time with other women, so he started hating him for that. Since our father doted on me this made me a bad person in Pierre's eyes. So he and I argued during much of our childhood, insulting each other and telling lies about the other to whichever parent would listen.

In 1932 when I was 8 years old my father went to New York by ship and then to Seattle by train. There he contacted some apple growers and they agreed to start shipping 'Delicious' apples to France—thus beginning a very lucrative importing business for him. In a short period of time, he was also importing pears, oranges and then fruit juices into France.

When his importing business made him very wealthy, we moved again, this time to Avenue Malakov, a very affluent section of Paris near the Arc de Triomphe and the Bois-de-Boulogne.

We had an 18 room apartment and I can still see it today—a very large entry and hallway, a huge living room and library and also a smaller living room for my piano, where my mother would receive her lady friends. Our dining room could easily accommodate 12 people and we also had five bedrooms, four and a half baths, a gigantic kitchen and a butler's pantry. There was also an exercise room or gym, a separate laundry, and four maids' rooms. My father's professional success funded a life of luxury, and since he preferred being with the Paris elites, we often hosted parties for very important people.

In addition, my father's success also allowed him dalliances with lots of women.

He made enough money to finance family cruises to North and South America as well as skiing in the Alps, but those were the only times he was with us. He essentially left us in 1936, when I was 12. My mother was devastated as he was her whole life. His leaving us traumatized me and resulted in my being insecure for the rest of my life.

Every so often he showed up and graced us with his presence. He would appear without notice bearing gifts for all of us and acting as if he had never left. No doubt he must have been in between mistresses then and each time my mother welcomed him home, certain this time he would stay.

Once he was gone for months without contacting us and one day he showed up in a taxi filled with flowers, telling my mother she would always be his only true love. During this visit my baby sister Poussy was conceived. When she was born my father was gone again and my poor mother had no money. My grandmother had to pay the hospital bill.

Money changed our lives completely. Sometimes the bills

were not paid and so the electricity was cut off. This roller-coaster existence further added to my insecurities.

Growing up, I often heard stories about my father's many mistresses—especially a Romanian-born French actress named Alice Cocéa. Much later in my life, with Catherine's help researching the Internet, I found a Wikipedia listing for Alice that claimed my father was her second husband. He is described as "a shady figure who rose from being a vegetable dealer to the head of a major newspaper in Paris during the Nazi Occupation and later a fascist-leaning theatrical figure."

For the record, the vegetable dealer reference is not the only factual error in this Wikipedia post. My father was never married to Alice Cocéa. She was just one of his many mistresses. He obviously didn't think that highly of her since he ended up fathering a child with her maid! I wanted Catherine to add this bit of salacious news to the Wikipedia posting but she declined to do it; she was only willing to change the "married" reference to "mistress."

During the early part of the 20th century, there was a recognized and even celebrated social class system in France. People with means lived differently from other folks, and having a mistress was a status symbol because it meant you could afford both a family and a mistress. In fact, it was common to always ask when inviting guests for dinner whether a man would bring his wife or his mistress. After all, the name tags had to be correct!

Since my father had made a fortune importing fruit, his mistress Alice wanted him to invest in the theater so he could produce plays for her. And to keep her, he agreed.

He directed five plays in which Alice Cocéa starred and that is why he is known as "a fascist-leaning theatrical producer" on Wikipedia. During the war, he became publisher of the Paris newspaper Dimanche Matin. He also became friends with Jean Cocteau, a well known French writer and filmmaker, and was rumored to have tricked him into reading his works, which my father then tape recorded and sold without his permission. There was no end to my father's ingenuity for making money in unusual ways, and to feel totally justified in breaking the rules.

In the summer of 1938, my father bought us a summer home that we called Lerina—a villa in Golfe-Juan across the street from the Mediterranean. It was my mother's consolation prize for his affair with Alice. Since he could now be alone in Paris every summer he could still carry on with his mistress even though he had promised my mother he would not see her again.

Five years later, my mother had to put Lerina in her children's names to keep it from being seized by my father's creditors. There was never a dull moment in our lives.

My mother didn't know that while she got the house, Alice the mistress received a consolation prize; a stunning Cartier jewel set including a ring, necklace, broche and bracelet in diamonds and rubies—to pacify her when she learned about my baby sister Poussy's birth. This gift would result in my brother Pierre spending a year in prison when the Nazis occupied Paris.

CHAPTER 4

ONCE UPON A WAR

CLAUDINE

I was only fourteen in June 1939 when I met Gabe who was much older at nineteen. I was spending the summer in Golfe-Juan at Lerina, our family's ocean-front home. It was fun being in this quaint fishing village in the South of France. What's not to like about crossing the street to swim in the Mediterranean? When I compared my life and friends in Paris to Golfe-Juan and its provincial residents; it was two different worlds.

This particular day my seventeen-year old brother Pierre was bored and he invited a neighbor to play bridge. This guy brought a friend, whose name was Gabe, and since they needed a fourth, Pierre begrudgingly asked me to join them. This surprised me because for most of my life Pierre had made it clear he thought I was an idiot and he rarely ever spent any time with me. So I was shocked he asked me to take part in this bridge game.

Pierre said I could play but I would have to keep my mouth shut. At first I did as I was told and just kept looking at my cards. It wasn't that I was shy; I just didn't want to give Pierre a reason to humiliate me as he often did in front of others.

Honestly, I don't remember much from that day but I can tell you I was not impressed with Gabe. Yes he was tall, handsome and had a good sense of humor but he lived in Golfe-Juan for God's sake! What could we possibly have in common?

I should also admit that even though I lived in Paris my exposure to boys or young men had been limited. In fact I was just six years old when Charlie Chaplin's oldest son Sidney kissed me. When we lived on the Avenue Malakov, Sidney and his brother Charles spent time with us when they were visiting their mother.

GABE

I got this invitation to play bridge and since I didn't have any plans that day, I thought what the hell? So my friend and I arrived at this grand, five story house across the street from the beach in Golfe-Juan and the maid showed us into the card room. My friend introduced me to Pierre—a very tan, somewhat diminutive guy with the most piercing blue eyes I'd ever seen. We made small talk and I decided I liked him. He amused me and was obviously a Parisian. We needed a fourth to play bridge so Pierre announced he'd get his kid sister to join us.

Now this part I remember very clearly. She came in walking behind Pierre and was even more diminutive than her brother; just five feet tall at most and probably weighed less than forty three kilos. She had these magnificent blue green eyes that looked like marbles, dark hair cut short and a golden French Riviera tan. She was also quite "stacked," if you know what I mean?

We all sat down and started playing. I was having a hard time concentrating on my hand; I couldn't stop looking at her. I was amazed she was only fourteen but she could hold her own with us older guys. She didn't say much but when she did talk it was obvious she was mature beyond her age. She also freely expressed an opinion, which in itself was unique since she was the only female in the group. I could tell this pissed her brother off and he regularly said to her

"Fèrme ta bouche" (shut your mouth)

Compared to the young ladies I knew in Golfe-Juan, she definitely had lived a different life. I was intrigued. Hell I think I fell in love with her that very day and I was determined to pursue her.

CLAUDINE

Since Golfe-Juan was such a small village, Gabe and I continued running into each other quite often that summer. We got to be very good friends but that's all, at least as far as I was concerned. By the middle of that summer, I became interested in local boys my age, none of whom were deemed proper enough by my mother. This meant they didn't come from "good" families (translation: money). That's where Gabe came in handy.

In order for me to be with these undesirables, I told my mother I was going out with Gabe —a young man heavily favored by my mother because of his impeccable family credentials. He would come to the house and we walked to the village up the street where I met my real date. Gabe would come back later to take me home so my mother would think we had been together all the time. This went on for the rest of the summer.

On September 3, 1939, while we were celebrating my 15th birthday in Golfe-Juan, the Nazis decided to invade Poland. So France declared war on Germany, on MY birthday! All of a sudden, everything changed and our lives were turned upside down for the next five years.

My mother left Pierre and me with the household staff and took a train to Paris to get clothes, silver, linens and a few other items from the apartment. Had she known then what would happen over the next twelve months, she would have made arrangements to take a lot more items out of that apartment.

Since we were now stuck in Golfe-Juan for who knew how long, I had to go to the public school there with kids I thought were rather backwards. Fortunately, I still had Gabe to rely on to get me out of the house once in a while. During the rest of 1939 and into the early part of 1940, we all thought the war would end quickly.

That notion ended when the Germans invaded Paris in June 1940. That's when we learned they had taken possession of our apartment and all of its contents. By July it also became too dangerous for us to stay in Golf-Juan so we went to Toulouse in southwestern France to live with my mother's brother. By then my father had totally abandoned us and my mother had no financial support.

I don't know how we survived. My mother had no skills so she couldn't get a job, and she was also incapable of managing a household and taking care of three kids. Thankfully her brother was more capable and he had a maid who cooked the meals and cleaned the house.

One day that fall my mother found out from a friend that her husband was living in a hotel on the Atlantic coast with a group of actors and actresses. She tracked him down just as he was driving into the hotel's parking lot. When he saw his wife and children, he was far more chagrined to be found than he was relieved we were still alive. When my mother told him we needed money, he said he could not help us as he was supporting actors and actresses.

That really got to me. I reached into in his car and grabbed his wallet. I took as much money as I could before he took it from me. He was furious with me but at least now we had some money to live on. This is just one example of how crazy life was during the war.

∾

GABE

Claudine is forgetting the best story! She should have talked about what happened to Pierre during the war!

While I was living my rather boring life in Golfe-Juan, the Capgras family in Toulouse added another crisis to their turbulent year. In the middle of all the turmoil Pierre received a letter from a woman named Jacqueline, telling him she was pregnant with his child. She was engaged to a friend of Pierre's, a Jean-Philippe whose last name I don't remember. Anyway she had been spending time in Provence with her grandparents and told her fiancé she was very bored. So he had asked Pierre to look in on her. Pierre graciously complied, evidently going a bit overboard. When Jacqueline's mother learned her daughter was pregnant, she insisted they get married. That's what people did in those days.

In France you had to be 18 to marry and Pierre was only 17. So he and Jacqueline lived in Paris with her family until he was 18 and then they were married. Their daughter Roselyne was born three months later.

That's not even the best part of this story! In addition to becoming a very young father, Pierre thought he didn't have enough to worry about so he joined the French resistance in Paris. He also decided that as his mother's only son he should help her financially, however he could. Since he had little money of his own, and few opportunities to earn any, he decided his father should contribute. When Pierre learned his father was no longer involved with the actress Alice Cocéa, he told him to get the Cartier jewels back from her, then sell them and give the money to his mother.

Unfortunately, Pierre was unaware that when Alice and Roger had gone separate ways, she had become the German ambassador's mistress. Somehow Alice learned Pierre had asked

Roger to take her jewels away, so out of spite she told her lover Pierre was one of the leaders in the French resistance.

Pierre was arrested, charged with multiple crimes and, at 18, sentenced to death.

CLAUDINE

Yes, Gabe is right. All of that happened to Pierre. Every day the Nazis would walk through the rows of prisoners and select one of them for execution. Pierre thought he would be chosen each time. Luckily, the Germans finally realized he was too young to have committed all the crimes he had been charged with so they released him. He was told never to set foot in Paris again.

Pierre was just 19 when he came out of prison; he had lost 30 pounds and all of his hair. He was bald for the rest of his life. Since he did not want to be sent to Germany for work detail, he hid until the war ended; relying on either family members or friends to shelter him. He had no means of supporting a family, so Jacqueline and Roselyne stayed with her family.

When the war ended, Pierre had no connections and so he was forced to work with our father— which must have been interesting since he hated him. At that time our father was a successful fruit dealer, working at the Halles of Paris. So it was an opportunity Pierre could not turn down; he had no other offers.

As predicted, Pierre and Jacqueline's marriage did not last long but she would always be the love of his life. Ironically, she divorced Pierre to marry another one of his friends— also named Jean-Philippe.

So there is one more story about the war. Pierre was not the only family member who suffered under the Nazis. My father was also imprisoned by the Germans near Grenoble, but once again he got lucky. He was among a group of French VIPs who escaped to North Africa when the Americans provided a submarine transport for them. When the war ended in 1945 my mother received a letter from the Red Cross that my father had been in a terrible car accident and was in a coma for weeks. There would be no more news from or about him for the next four years.

CHAPTER 5

MY SUIT GOT THERE FIRST

CLAUDINE

In 1941, when I was 17, I decided I could no longer live under Nazi rule. At the time, I was in public school in Golfe-Juan trying to finish my diploma in spite of the war. When I learned my Jewish friend Roland Veil was leaving for England I decided to go with him. However, in order for me to go with him, we had to be married. The legal age to marry was still 18, so I needed one parent's consent.

My mother understood why I wanted to leave France but she was totally against my marrying Roland. I was pretty stubborn about this and kept arguing with her. She already had enough on her plate to worry about—Pierre was imprisoned by the Nazis and her husband was missing—but she ultimately agreed to sign the consent form just to get me off her back. In order to really understand what a bad decision we both had made; Roland was Jewish! The Nazis and my father had created so much stress for my mother, she wasn't thinking right. So Roland and I got married!

GABE

For the record, I also tried very hard to talk Claudine out of marrying Roland. This was not just a ridiculous choice—to marry someone just to get out of the country—but she also chose a Jew, during World War II! I had nothing against Roland, you understand, in fact we were friends but I thought she was totally irrational about doing this to get away from the Nazis.

Oh, and they didn't just elope. I don't recall whose idea this was but they actually had a formal wedding to commemorate the "happy" occasion! There is a beautiful photo of Claudine in a wedding gown, leaning against the balcony at Lerina. She looked radiant with happiness in that photo. For years our children assumed this was our wedding day, because we told them it was. But it was the day she married Roland.

Now here's the funny part – and I LOVE to tell this story! Poor Roland didn't have a pot to piss in and could not afford a proper suit for the wedding. Naturally, Claudine asked me if he could borrow one of my suits since we were the same size. So I loaned him a blue suit for the occasion.

As far as I'm concerned this means I actually married Claudine twice – first she married my suit and then she married me!

At the wedding, I had a lot to drink. Even though I knew she was only marrying him to get out of France, I thought my chances with her were gone. I joked that since she was taken, I would have to wait for her younger sister Poussy to grow up. Thank God that never happened; it would have been a colossal mistake.

CLAUDINE

Initially, Roland and I tried to go to England by way of Spain but that failed since the Germans had already infiltrated that country. Since we had to stay in France, we wanted to be useful so like Pierre we joined the resistance in Paris.

The next three years or so are a blur and I think I've consciously blocked out much of what happened. We were constantly running from the Nazis and Roland and I never really lived together. He rose quickly in the ranks of the Resistance so the Gestapo was after him. Since my last name was now Veil, a very Jewish family name, I had to obtain fake papers in order to get around. For much of those three years, we kept moving around France, bunking in with friends. The only thing I remember is we were always hungry.

So I had little excitement during the war, except when it finally started coming to an end. When the Allies landed in Normandy on D Day, June 6, 1944 our resistance group was sent to Argenton near Paris to hide until the city could be liberated. That August 1944 I was living with a friend in the small village of La Ferte-Alais, just south of Paris, while Roland was hiding in the forest with his resistance group.

Each night I would sneak out to the woods and give them information about the Nazis' activities in the village and updates on how the allies were advancing in Normandy.

One night the resistance attacked the Germans, causing some serious casualties. The Nazis decided to get even. First they gathered up all the men in the village and sent them all away; we assumed to concentration camps. Then they rounded up all the women and asked to see our papers. I had to show them a set of obviously-doctored papers. I was shaking so hard my teeth were clicking and I started feeling nauseous. They lined me up along with several other women in town who had similar fake papers.

My parents had not practiced a religion so I had never prayed, but I started to ask God to spare me.

Moments later a small group of Germans was facing us and I realized they were a firing squad. I almost fainted; my entire body was now shaking and I thought I would vomit. Suddenly a wounded German officer appeared and asked me how old I was.

When I told him I was 20 years old, he said I was too young and too pretty to die so he told me to run. This would not be the only time my life was spared.

When the war ended, Roland and I went our separate ways. I moved back to Golfe-Juan because my family had returned to Lerina. Although our Paris apartment no longer was held by the Germans, we were not able to save it from my father's creditors. They took everything.

There was never any romantic attachment between Roland and me. He was a friend and I thought he could provide a way out of the country. When we parted that day, it didn't matter if I ever saw him again. I assumed he felt the same way.

Years later, Roland's name came up in a conversation, which served to confirm that France is a small country.

In 1952 Pierre's second wife Aglaé and I were on the balcony at Lerina talking about our experiences during the war. I just happened to mention that Roland had been pretty high up in the Paris resistance and Aglaé said her first husband also was very involved in the French resistance. His code name was Marco Polo. Then she told me he was captured by the Germans the day he was supposed to meet another resistance fighter whose code name was Orphée on a Sunday in June at the Luxembourg gardens in Paris.

I could not believe what I was hearing! Roland, whose code name was Orphée had told me about that failed meeting at the Luxembourg gardens. He had gone to meet Marco Polo, but when he got to the designated spot, he saw someone being arrested by the Gestapo—and he assumed it was Marco Polo! Only in a small country like France could you find these coincidences!

CHAPTER 6

TOGETHER AT LAST

GABE

During the two years Claudine and Roland were hiding from the Nazis, I was living in Golfe-Juan and had started working with my two cousins in a perfume business in Vallauris. I thought of her often and hoped she would come to her senses and leave Roland once the war was over. We exchanged letters whenever we could, but since she didn't have a permanent home it was hard to keep up with her. I could tell from her letters, she still only thought of me as a pal, just someone to write to.

Finally the blasted war ended, thanks to the Allies, and Claudine wrote that she was coming back to Golfe-Juan, alone. I feared that during her time with Roland she had fallen in love with him, but since she was coming back alone, I was hopeful. The day after she arrived in Golfe-Juan I went to Lerina to see her. She had matured quite a bit during those two years and was now a young woman; even more opinionated. She told me all about the hideouts where they lived, her connections in the Resistance and about the time she was nearly killed by Nazis. I was most elated to learn Roland had gone his separate way, and they were no longer a couple.

In addition to having matured, she also had become even more beautiful. Her crystal blue and green eyes were more pronounced than I remembered. She was funny, almost outrageous at times, and she was always ready to have a good time. I loved every minute I spent with her.

A couple of months later I asked her if she would be divorcing Roland, trying not to show urgency in my voice. I was not ready to divulge my real reason for asking about it. She didn't seem to catch on so I decided I would not rush it. I did not want to lose her again.

CLAUDINE

Gabe had been acting strange ever since I had returned to Golfe-Juan. I didn't know if it was because we hadn't seen each other for a couple of years or if something had changed with him. I think he was trying to be subtle, but I began to suspect he might want to be more than a friend. I mentioned this to my mother and she laughed and said it was obvious to her and the rest of the family that he had always wanted to be more than a friend.

Then we went out to dinner one night—it was May 2, I'm sure—and as we were driving to the restaurant, I couldn't wait any longer and I said to him

"Alors, tu m'aime?" (So do you love me?)

Instead of answering, he pulls the car over to the side of the road and says to me:

"I have been in love with you since 1939."In English, not in French! I was so stunned about hearing this that it wasn't until much later that I realized how strange it was for him to answer in English. Was he too nervous to admit it in French?

So that's the night we started out the evening as friends and came home in love. We have both chosen not to provide additional details on that memorable night, but May 2 has always been our official anniversary even though we didn't get married until October 1947. After that night we knew we were meant to be together. He started calling me "Minette," which is the name of a small Italian bird and that would become my nickname. I mostly called him Gabe or Gaby. In later years, I used Gabriel more often when he made me angry.

I had never been in love before, so I didn't know if my feelings for him were normal but all I wanted to do was spend every minute of the day with him. Of course that was not possible since he had a job at the perfume business, but we were together many evenings and every weekend. One day I met one of his friends, and he said:

"Ah, finally I meet the little green-eyed girl Gabe has been panting for all this time."

Claudine in Golfe-Juan, circa 1945

That's when I knew all this time he had wanted me. When he begged me not to marry Roland, it wasn't just because he knew it was crazy for me to marry a Jewish man during the Nazi occupation. It was that, yes, but now I knew it was also because he loved me. Then I thought back to the day I married Roland and I overheard Gabe tell my brother that now he would have to wait for my sister Poussy. Why didn't I get it then? I must have been very naïve.

By June we decided to get married. That meant I had to get a divorce. So I got in touch with Roland's former resistance friends and managed to get his address. I sent him a letter telling him Gabe and I were going to be married so I wanted a divorce. Although Roland knew I only married him to get out of the country, he said he would not give me a divorce! I was stunned and thought the only possible reason was that he needed money and expected to tap into my family's money. That was a joke because by this time our house Lerina was the only asset we had left.

We were desperate to find a way around this dilemma and asked various people what our options were. Our friend Pierre Chassin told us all we had to do was to get caught in bed and that would be grounds. With the help of a policeman friend, we staged such a scene and brought the evidence to Roland. Still he refused to grant me a divorce. We were devastated.

So we did the only other thing we thought would work. We decided I would get pregnant and Roland would surely reconsider. Even after Marie-Anne was born, Roland refused to give me that divorce. Then I got pregnant with Catherine soon after Marie-Anne was born, and still Roland refused to let me go. France was so backward then, when the girls were born their birth certificates list Gabriel Raphel as the father but the mother as "unknown" because we were no married. Finally four years and two children later, Roland—always referred to as "the suit" by Gabe—finally agreed to a divorce. Since I had no money Gabe had to pay for it and we were married in October of 1947.

GABE

Once Claudine learned she was pregnant, we had to find housing for our growing family. Just before Marie-Anne was born in April 1946, we moved out of the very small cottage we had been renting in Golfe-Juan and got settled into L'Oustalet—her uncle Charles and aunt Zaza's winter home in the village. Our second daughter Catherine was born the following year in May.

By then I was working in a perfume business in Vallauris with two of my cousins; Jacqueline and Jean. We had issues from the start. They were quite a bit older than me and they did not share my new idea to expand the business by producing essential oils. Also, their facility lacked the equipment to extract the scent from flowers such as jasmine and rose, and I really wanted to get into this side of the perfume business. I believed this would yield the most profit. I was determined to make a lot of money, very quickly.

In 1950 I decided I had to branch out on my own if I wanted to reach my aggressive business goals. I sold my share of the perfume business in Vallauris and started my operation in Golfe-Juan with the proceeds.

Gabe in Golfe-Juan, circa 1949

Here again, I got lucky. My family owned a number of buildings across the street from Juliette-Antoinette. Those buildings once had been used for some kind of manufacturing but had been idle for years. This included office space, a substantial storage area with a small apartment on top of that and a large apartment directly over the main factory. Since I didn't have to pay for this space, I was able to invest heavily in the equipment necessary to produce essential oils. This allowed me to grow that side of the business very rapidly.

My business did not include creating scents for fine fragrances. Instead, it was made up of two parts: one was the distillation and extraction of natural plants and flowers such as jasmine or rose, then processing them for sale. The other part of the business was purchasing and reselling essential oils.

At the beginning of the winter of 1950 Charles and Zaza told us they wanted to move back into L'Oustalet. That's when we moved into the large apartment above the factory. By this time, the business was booming—especially the essential oils part—and we were able to hire a maid. That's when Madeleine came into our lives.

CLAUDINE

Life was so good to us then. Gabe and I were very much in love and thrilled to be parents. Our daughter Marie-Anne had a difficult first year as a result of drinking spoiled condensed milk. There was a lot of that going on right after the war; food was often contaminated. She was never hungry because of that and she was so thin we worried constantly about her health. I can still remember the hours Gabe and I spent trying to get her to eat, pleading with her but she just kept her mouth tightly shut.

Catherine was another story—we couldn't feed her enough

and soon she was heavier than her older sister. It was difficult having two babies born thirteen months apart but now that Gabe's business was doing so well we could afford a nanny who helped me a few days a week.

We had a lot of friends in Golfe-Juan who were also doing well financially and they were always ready to enjoy the night life with us. We often took day trips to Monaco or Provence on the weekends, and occasionally went to Paris by train. Since both my mother Charlotte and my aunt Zaza lived nearby, it was not a problem to leave the girls with them. Gabe had not spent much time in Paris and I was very happy to show him the city, especially the location of our fancy apartment and my private school. We also spent time with Pierre who was finally able to return to Paris and live with Jacqueline and Roselyne.

Whenever I think back to those days, I can't help but remember the night we went out to dinner to celebrate a perfumer's award Gabe had won. It was in the spring of 1949 and he decided we should go to a very fancy restaurant in Cannes. We dressed in our finest clothes—I thought we looked like movie stars! We even hired a driver with a fancy car to bring us to the restaurant.

When we arrived the Maitre D thought we were either movie stars or royalty. He met us at the door with great enthusiasm and led us to the best table in the house. We were immediately served glasses of very good Champagne and the waiter kept going on and on about how thrilled they were to have us as guests that evening.

Halfway through the meal, Gabe pulls out an envelope from his suit pocket and tells me he has a discount coupon for this restaurant. This was given to him because of that award. Well, you can imagine my reaction! I was thoroughly enjoying the celebrity status, so I did NOT want him to use that coupon to pay for our meal. That would certainly give us away as anything BUT celebrities.

"Gabriel, je t'en pris! Je ne veux pa que tu te serve de ce

coupon de réduction!" (Gabe, please! I don't want you to use the coupon!)

Well he used the coupon and I was not happy about that! Here I had been treated like a queen all evening and now we were going to be found out. Every time Gabe tells this story, he still thinks it's hilarious. I was not amused.

CHAPTER 7

CHILDHOOD MEMORIES

CATHERINE

Now that I have joined this family I will tell you about two people who mattered most to me when I was growing up in Golfe-Juan; one is my sister Marie-Anne and the other is our maid Madeleine. I have retained some memories of those early years, supported by faded black and white photos. Family members also helped me recall some of these moments.

My sister Marie-Anne was born in April 1946, just one year after the end of the Second World War. I was born in May 1947 and that's when my parents moved into L'Oustalet, Zaza and Charles' winter home in Golfe-Juan. This was a temporary situation, I was later told, until my parents could find something more permanent. As it turned out, we were in that house nearly three years.

Capgras family in front of L'Oustalet, 1948. First row, left to right: Poussy, Roselyne, Catherine in carriage, Mamie Charlotte holding Marie-Anne. Second row: Claudine and Pierre.

In some of the family pictures, I look much heavier than Marie-Anne and it's not just because I ate too much. When she was an infant, she drank some spoiled milk from a can. My mother told me canned evaporated milk was the only milk available after the war. The bad milk made my sister nauseous for a long time and she would not eat. So that affected her growth. Today that's called "failure to thrive". Getting her to eat was a chore, I was told. She could only stomach certain foods and even when she liked something she hardly ate at all, even with pleas and bribes from our parents and our nanny. Marie-Anne was very skinny as a toddler and would be thin for the rest of her life.

Marie-Anne, left, and Catherine at L'Oustalet, 1948

In old family photos her legs were half the size of mine even though I was thirteen months younger. In fact, I was so chunky I did not walk until I was almost two years old. That's how I earned the nickname "Tounie," shortened version of "La Grosse Toune," (the fat ton) to highlight my girth. Somehow, Marie-Anne got the nickname "mayonnaise" which quickly got shortened to "Mayou,"

Since I'm on the topic of nicknames, we never called our parents Maman and Papa, as most French kids did. Somehow our mother became Mounette (an off shout of Minette, the pet name my father used perhaps?) and our father was always Doddy (not Daddy). Both of those nicknames ended when Marie-Anne and I got to America, but that comes much later.

Catherine and Marie-Anne, 1950

As little girls we were always dressed alike. The only exception was the year I was six and Marie-Anne was seven. There was a fancy costume ball in Nice and we went dressed as a couple from Holland. Since I was the bigger one, I was the man and so I wore pants that day.

Catherine. Left, and Marie-Anne at the Nice costume ball, 1953

Aside from how we were dressed, we were close in our early years but also competitive; so we were typical siblings. I was told I looked a lot like my Aunt Poussy (whom we nicknamed Tante Pest – Aunt Pest, and she wore that name well) while Marie-Anne favored our father's cousin Jacqueline, with whom he had earlier worked in the perfume business. Aside from our physical differences, our personalities were radically different—she was very reserved and shy, whereas I was outrageous and opinionated.

Catherine and Marie-Anne, 1950

Marie-Anne was not typical of first born children who often have large personalities but I was what you'd expect from a second child of the same sex—always trying to make up for not being a different gender.

Now let me tell you about my Madeleine.

She came to work for us when I was just 18 months old, initially just during the day. We also had our nanny NouNou, but she only came part time when Mounette had social engagements. Madeleine cooked, cleaned and kept me company; she did such a good job she was invited to come live with us soon after she started.

I spent many hours in the kitchen of L'Oustalet with Madeleine, which probably explains how I got chubby. She held me in one arm so she could stir whatever was on the stove. I credit Madeleine for my love of good food and life-long interest in cooking. I was especially fond of her over-sized crepes. Once, I'm told, I ate eight of these crepes and my parents were shocked I didn't have a major case of indigestion.

Madeleine was a big woman (which is how she could hold me in just one arm while she stirred). She was tall, husky and had hair on her face. Since she smoked a lot her voice was raspy, kind of like a man, and often she coughed. Her smoking habit meant she smelled like a cigarette since she chose Gitannes, the very strong unfiltered cigarettes. None of that ever mattered to me. I adored her, loved hearing her stories and laughing with her. Madeleine never had children and I think she pretended I was her daughter.

The only strong memory I have of our life in L'Oustalet, is the day my tonsils were taken out in the living room while I was strapped in a barber's chair. It's really a very fleeting memory but Mounette talked about it so often it became ingrained in my sub-conscience. I was only three years old when our family doctor told my parents I would continue getting tonsillitis until my tonsils came out. Somehow this doctor convinced my parents it would be easier to do the surgery at home rather than at a hospital. The doctor assured my parents it was minor surgery and I would feel nothing. For the rest of her life, Mounette would recall the day this took place, in the living room of L'Oustalet, and that she could still hear my screams years later. Madeleine almost quit that day; she was that horrified by what took place. She only stayed to protect me from further abuse, she said.

I know I spent much of my childhood in Golfe-Juan with Madeleine, rather than with Mounette. As far as Madeleine was concerned, I could do no wrong and she thought I was the funniest child that ever lived

For instance, I could burp and fart in front of Madeleine and she never got angry at me like Mounette did. Mostly, she just let me be ME, but she did teach me about proper etiquette as it related to bathroom activities. When I was going through potty training, I would yell out to her:

"Madeleine J'ai besoin de faire popo" ("I need to poop"). She told me it was fine to say this at home but not fine at all when I was around other people. Then I had to say:

"J'ai besoin d'aller au petit coin." ("I need to go to the little corner.")

The French were very proper then—toilet was changed to corner, at least in my world.

Madeleine did yell at me once—the day she invited me to the house she still kept in Vallauris. I must have been about six years old then. There were three boys about my age playing in the courtyard and I went to join them. Since there was little to do the boys started a contest to see who could pee the highest against a wall. Thinking I could also compete, I proceeded to take my pants off and attempted to pee along with them. Madeleine came out of the house screaming, pulled up my pants and dragged me into her house. She said girls are not made to pee with boys and that she would not tell my mother or I would get punished. I loved her even more. I suppose that was the beginning of my life-long attempts at competing with boys.

To further emphasize Madeleine's role in my life, more than six decades later I named our South Carolina house "La Madeleine" in her honor. When my mother came to visit she couldn't understand why I named the only house I ever built after our maid. This served to remind me again of all those hours I spent with Madeleine and not with her.

Unfortunately, no one took a picture of the two of us together. When many years later I asked my mother if there was such a picture, she told me "it wasn't done then to take pictures of the help." This amazed and angered me. Madeleine wasn't "the help"; she was my confidant and protector.

When Marie-Anne was five and started school in Golfe-Juan, it was soon obvious that she would not do well in that environment. She was extremely shy, would not participate in any school activity and barely spoke to the teacher. By Christmas Mounette was beside herself worrying about her. She met with her teacher who suggested sending me to school with her to help overcome her shyness.

Catherine and Marie-Anne at L'Oustalet, 1950

That's why I started school as a four year old and soon Marie-Anne was talking and participating in activities. When the school year ended, the teacher told my parents I could handle moving up to the next grade.

For the rest of our school years, Marie-Anne and I remained in the same grade. The following year, we were sent to Sainte Marie de Chavagne, a Catholic school in Cannes dating back to

1879, where our grandmother Juliette had gone to school. Our uncle Claude, whose emotional difficulties you heard about from Doddy, could not keep a job so he became our chauffeur.

Even though the Catholic school was supposed to be more advanced than the public school, I started bringing home some rather impressive grades (they called them "marques" in France). Halfway through the year, I asked Doddy what he would buy for me if I ended up first in the class at the end of the year. He told me he would buy me anything I wanted. When I did clinch the top spot in the class all I wanted was a large box of coloring pencils. My parents made such a big deal of my school performance that I feared they might expect this from that point on. To curb that expectation, I became an average student for the next sixteen years and only got top grades again once I got to graduate school.

At about this time Zaza and Charles told my parents they wanted to live in L'Oustalet again during the winter. That's when we moved to an apartment above the factory, across the street from Juliette-Antoinette where Doddy's mother, brother and sister lived. Things were fine for a while but then Marie-Anne started getting very nauseous when Doddy was distilling flowers in April and August—releasing pungent scents. The doctor told us the spoiled milk issue might have affected her kidneys and could be causing her nausea. Whatever the cause, she was eating even less. It became clear we had to find somewhere else to live, away from the scents.

The move also became urgent when a large open window framed in metal put a hole in my head. I was bending down to grab a toy on the floor and I stood up against the corner of that window. As could be expected, my head bled profusely. I can still recall Madeleine holding me in her arms as she applied a towel to the wound. This required a hospital visit, and my first experience with stitches.

We weren't in that apartment very long, but I have another

vivid memory of the large storage area that held mountains of rose petals. Marie-Anne and I would take off our shoes and jump into the pile to see which one of us could jump the highest and then disappear into the roses. We would do this repeatedly until we came across the hannetons—flying creatures similar to beetles—and then we would run out of there screaming as if they were snakes.

When our parents needed to find another place to live, Charles and Zaza offered them a piece of land in Vallauris, next to their summer home called Le Pin Pignou. At this time, my grandmother Juliette was living across the street from our apartment in Juliette-Antoinette. When she heard her favorite child might no longer be living across the street, she quickly offered us the house and agreed to live in the apartment.

Although Mounette was not excited about continuing to live across the street from her mother-in-law, Juliette-Antoinette was too tempting to refuse.

"Living so close to my mother in law was not ideal," Mounette told me more than once. "Juliette was very devoted to Gabe and she would come every morning to talk to him while he ate breakfast. She also made Madeleine furious by regularly re-arranging Gabe's clothes drying on the line because she didn't like the way the maid had hung them up."

The house needed quite a bit of work but since the business was booming, my parents could afford the renovations. They put in a brand new kitchen and heating system and added a veranda above the existing terrace. Once the interior was thoroughly cleaned and painted, we moved into Juliette-Antoinette late in 1953.

Since I was only six, I have just a few memories of the house. One of them is the small vineyard in the lower garden. Once the grapes were ready to be picked, they went into a very deep wooden barrel and Doddy stepped in it. Then he grabbed me and put me in the barrel with him and we stomped those grapes into wine. I am not making this up. I also have very fond memories of the bedroom I shared with Marie-Anne that had French doors that led to a balcony where you could see the sea below. The view was terrific and even as a child I thought it was rather cool to have the sea so close to our house. I tended to do some sleep walking then and my parents were concerned one day I would fall from the balcony, but that never happened.

Catherine and Marie-Anne in Juliette-Antoinette, 1954

Doddy was fixated on flies. It made him crazy that so many of them came into the house every time someone forgot to close a door or a window. There weren't screens on the windows back then so in the summer we had large nets around our beds to keep out the bugs at night. When Doddy would see a fly, he would chase after each invader with whatever article of destruction he found—a folded newspaper, a slipper and even a broom when he was desperate. Every time he killed a fly he would yell:

"Son cadavre sinistre en poussière est tomber!" (Its sinister cadaver fell as dust).

I suspect he read this in a history book that focused on war, but I'm sure it was referring to people not flies.

Once we were well settled in Juliette-Antoinette our parents decided we needed dogs in our family and we welcomed Taki; a large copper-colored standard dachshund. He was soon joined by two females; Bunny, who became my dog, and Anouk who was Doddy's favorite dog. Although we hadn't planned to breed the females, they both came into heat at the same time and somehow we failed to take note of this. It did not escape Taki, however, who serviced them both well. Soon they each delivered eight squiggly puppies who delighted all of us and for whom we shed tears as one after another of our friends adopted them. As a consolation to losing our "babies," our parents allowed the adult dogs to sleep in our beds. Thus began my life-long habit of sleeping with dogs.

As the perfume business kept growing, so did my parents' flamboyant lifestyle. The small French cars were replaced by big fancy American cars, either Cadillac or Oldsmobile for Doddy, and a station wagon for Mounette. The antiques kept multiplying and the staff now included a gardener. Our clothes were all custom-made in Cannes by a tailor recommended by one of Mounette's friends. As each new large purchase came to the house, Doddy would say in a very loud voice:

"ABONDANCE!!" ("Abundance")

When my parents went out at night, which they did often, they got really dressed up. People did that then. I would sit on the bathtub and watch Mounette put on her makeup. I never understood how she could use an eye lash curler because it seemed like torture to me. She had very dark, thick lashes and they stood out even more when she curled them. Plus she had those large blue/green marble-like eyes that were magnificent. She always wore a bright color evening gown made of either satin or silk. It was gathered tightly at her tiny waste but had that off the shoulders look that really accentuated her little neck. The gown was even more dramatic because she also wore a stiff petticoat. I thought she looked like a princess. She always wore a shawl, which doubled as a scarf when she got into the convertible car. She was beautiful.

Doddy also looked extremely chic in a tuxedo, with a starched white shirt and shiny black shoes where I could see my reflection. He was tall and handsome, a prince really, and always ready well before Mounette but he would wait downstairs, very patiently. Finally, he would yell up to her:

"Minette, on va étre en retard!" ("Minette, we are going to be late) And she would roll her eyes up and yell back:

"Oui, j'arrive. Donne moi une autre minute!" ("Yes, I'm coming. Give me another minute") and for most of their life together he referred to her as "Last minute Minette."

In the summer of 1954 our parents sent Marie-Anne and me to San Pietro di Monterosso in Italy with Nounou. I don't recall where this little town was located but I do remember it involved a long car ride on very twisted roads and I got very car sick. It was in the mountains but not too far from the sea so it must have been in the southern part of the country. I don't remember much of that summer but I know I liked being there. I met new kids and I learned to speak Italian. If we had continued going there every summer, I suspect I would have been bi-lingual.

I had hoped Madeleine could come with us to Italy but Mounette said they needed her at home to cook and clean for them. In our absence, they had an elaborate house warming party so their friends could see how well they were doing. At least we got the topping on the cake.

They came to visit us every other weekend in Italy. During one of those visits I asked Mounette why they sent us to Italy while they stayed in France.

"Because it's not good for you and Marie-Anne to breathe the Mediterranean salt air all year long," Mounette replied with authority. Since I had acquired a bit of an attitude even at a young age, I asked her:

"How come the salt air isn't bad for you and Doddy?" I don't recall her answer but I doubt I accepted it.

After each of these visits, they would spend a couple of days in Venice or in Lake Como, always staying at the <u>Villa d'Este</u>. Formerly a residence for aristocrats, it has been a five star resort since 1873; one of the most celebrated in the world.

When Doddy was not traveling to Paris for business, he devoted a lot of time to sailing his Cape Dory – named The Georgian – in the Mediterranean. If there was not enough wind for a sail, there was always a friend's yacht to take them to Portofino or St. Tropez. Mounette sometimes accompanied him or she spent time with her mother, shopping in Cannes and having tea at Rohr's, an extravagant pastry shop. Marie-Anne and I would sometimes go with them and I can still see the impressive displays of cakes, tarts, cookies and breads.

"It was truly the "Days of Wine and Roses," Doddy recalled years later when he talked about that time in our lives. We had it all, and there was every reason to believe it would last forever; or so we thought.

Even my grandfather Roger, who hadn't been heard from in seven years, suddenly reappeared in Golfe-Juan and spent a few hours with us at Juliette-Antoinette. All this time I thought I only had one grandfather and suddenly this stranger appeared. I remember little from his visit, other than his very blue piercing eyes that greeted me when he came into the house. When Mounette recalled that visit she said she got the nerve to ask him why he had abandoned his family all those years ago.

"There are two kinds of people who matter to me—those who serve me and those who amuse me—and you don't belong to either category," he gave her as a logical explanation. That pretty much explains why Mounette never spoke kindly about her father.

Marie-Anne and I were very spoiled; we got anything we wanted. I started piano lessons and she and I signed up for ballet. I still remember the costume we wore for our first recital, at the Casino in Cannes (where they now hold the Film Festival). We were dressed as elves, with bright copper satin suits and green netting around the wrists and neck. We had tall pointed hats filled with paper to keep them up straight. There must have been 20 little girls on that stage when suddenly one of them lost her hat. Mounette didn't have to look twice before telling Doddy I was the one who had lost her hat. Either I was too energetic in my dance moves or maybe I had refused to stand still so my hat could be affixed firmly on my head. It's also possible I intentionally showed off so everyone would notice me.

My best friend in Golfe-Juan was Catherine Junot, the daughter of very good friends of our parents; everyone called her Kaki. Although she was several years older than me we often got together when our mothers had tea. Kaki had an older brother named Philippe Junot who many years later earned a lot of press by first marrying Princess Caroline of Monaco and then by being known as the French playboy who broke her heart. My cousin Roselyne, my Uncle Pierre's daughter, once had a huge crush on him but her parents forbade her to see him because he was such a playboy.

Philippe Junot was not the only "celebrity" who crossed our path when we lived in France. Pablo Picasso was living in Vallauris in the 1950s, and is often credited with elevating the town as the pottery center of the world. One day Picasso came into my great uncle and aunt's ceramic shop and asked if they would make a set of dishes for him, based on one of his designs. When the artist came back to pick up his dishes, he mentioned he was looking for a boxer puppy. He was thrilled to learn my great uncle Charles' boxer just had a litter. I'm told I was at the house the day he came to select his puppy, and that I got to meet him and even shook his hand. Sadly, I have no recollection of this as I was barely three years old.

Finally, another clear memory I have of my time in Golfe-Juan is having a meal at Tetou, a restaurant on the beach, made famous for its bouillabaisse. One time when we were there celebrating a birthday; Zaza and Charles had joined us. As we were crossing the street to get to our cars after our meal, Zaza — who had eaten too much — opened her blouse and removed her tight corset in view of everyone on the street.

Years later, I learned my paternal great-grandfather had purchased a small structure on that beach so his family could put on their suits before going into the water. It was not proper then to wear a bathing suit prior to being on the beach. My grandfather ultimately sold this structure to Ernest "Tetou" Cirio in 1918, and he opened the restaurant on this spot.

Because it was so close to Cannes and its famous Film Festival, Tetou became a "must dine" spot for Hollywood's A-list, including Angelina Jolie, Brad Pitt, Jack Nicholson and Robert De Niro. Sadly Tetou and two other restaurants on that beach were bulldozed in June 2018 because they all had been built illegally on public land. When I told my mother Tetou was gone, she was stunned.

"No one cared about who owned the land. You bought a structure and you assumed the land came with it. I'm sure your father's relative thought the land was his" she explained.

As you can see, life was very good for the Raphel family in Golfe Juan in the early fifties and none of us could have imagined this happiness would ever end.

CHAPTER 8

GABE'S WATERLOO

GABE

By early 1954 my essential oils business had grown so much I began thinking about hiring someone to manage my suppliers. Even though this was a critical part of my business, it's what I least liked to do. It required putting up with some difficult individuals, and it involved working with numbers and that had always been a chore for me.

Somebody must have been reading my mind because all of a sudden this Grassois perfumer named Marcus Roma appeared at my door. He introduced himself as a friendly competitor and told me he wanted to repay a debt he owed my grandfather. According to Roma my grandfather had loaned him 4,000 gold francs, which allowed him to start his lucrative perfume business. So that's why he now wanted to help me in some way.

At the time I never thought it was fishy. I only saw it as an opportune event, so I told him I had been thinking about hiring an operations guy. Roma appeared so believable that I actually thought he wanted to help me find the right person to hire. It never occurred to me that I should check this guy out. I did ask my mother whether she remembered if her father in law had ever loaned this guy any money.

Although my mother did not recall this old debt, I was anxious to rely on Roma because he was offering a quick fix to my pressing need. So when he advised me to turn over a critical part of my business to a stranger, I was more than happy to go along with this idea. Roma strongly recommended that I hire Paul Begetta, an astute business man he insisted had all the necessary connections and impeccable credentials.

I was young, arrogant and, yet, quite ignorant at the time. Had I checked, I would have learned Roma was far from a friendly competitor. In fact, he was very unhappy about my expansion in the essential oils business. During the German occupation, Roma had allocated the quantities of flowers sold to perfume companies and so he knew a lot of details about everyone's business. When he learned that I was manufacturing large quantities of product even though I had a small quota, he assumed I was circumventing his authority—and stealing business from him and his perfumer friends in Grasse. These perfumers had a reputation for destroying competitors; a fact I knew very well.

Aside from this lack of due diligence, I also ignored warnings from two good friends who were in the business. They told me the Grassois perfumers had recently put out of business a competitor who specialized in lavenders.

But I thought I knew it all and frankly I just didn't want to spend the time researching candidates to interview. I needed someone right away because I had too much to do and not enough time. As I look back on this now, I also placed too much value on my free time; I didn't want to work too many hours. So I hired Begetta for this very important position, and I gladly removed myself from that key part of my business.

He came on board and immediately identified the right suppliers and began building relationships with them. This allowed me to concentrate on other more gratifying parts of the business.

Through much of 1954, I committed to purchasing a significant amount of merchandise necessary to grow the business. I simply signed many blank checks so that Begetta could purchase the merchandise. Begetta told me he would keep all of the merchandise in his warehouses for safekeeping. As a result, I thought I had large quantities of merchandise warehoused in Nice under the careful supervision of my new employee. It never dawned on me to check on Begetta, to make sure he was doing as he promised.

All I cared about was that now I could focus only on those aspects of perfumery that interested me. Just as important, now I had more free time to sail my Cape Dory, travel to Monaco or Lake Como and spend time with family and friends. The French didn't work long hours like the Americans, and this had been confirmed often as I watched how little my father and his father before him had worked.

No one in our family, most of all me, was prepared for what happened later that year. One afternoon in November 1954, the phone rang at the factory and this is what I heard:

"Are you aware of the fact that your man Begetta has left the country and gone to Peru?"

I was so stunned to hear this I never even thought to ask for this guy's name. There was no reason for Begetta to go to Peru; nor had he told me that he planned to go there. The stranger repeated his words, thinking perhaps I had not heard him correctly.

I was in such a panicked state I was incoherent but told him I was not aware of this. Taking advantage of my shock the stranger then started suggesting some very suspicious next steps for me.

"Whatever you do, don't cancel your planned business trip to Paris tomorrow," he told me. That certainly should have been a tip off. How did he know I had this trip planned?

"And don't take any phone calls from anyone connected with Begetta," he added.

"Also, stay in a hotel for several days rather than go home," he urged. Later I realized that was so friends or suppliers would not be able to contact me.

I replayed that conversation in my mind for months. I finally came to the conclusion that because I was in shock, I was incapable of thinking or acting rationally. I ultimately realized this stranger was just one of several individuals who took part in a well-orchestrated sting to destroy my business.

In a couple of days, I was able to confirm Begetta had indeed left the country, taking with him millions of francs he had withdrawn from my business account during the many months I was giving him blank checks. There was not a speck of merchandise anywhere—nor were there any of the warehouses he had claimed to own. Instead of having impeccable credentials, I learned Begetta was a crook who owed hundreds of millions of francs to several local banks who gave him good references in the hopes of collecting what he owed them. They, too, were taken in by this man or perhaps they were part of the sting.

CLAUDINE

I will always remember that November day in 1954. Gabe came into the house from the factory and he looked like he'd just seen a ghost. He was so hysterical he couldn't even speak properly. When he finally told me about that stranger's phone call, I started screaming and crying at the same time. I have never been good at hiding my emotions. I tend to go overboard when bad things happen, and I consider most unexpected events as disasters. This is most likely because I had a difficult childhood with an unreliable father who often left us without any financial support. I kept saying over and over again:

"Mais non, ce n'est pas possible!" (But no, that's not possible!)

But Gabe kept telling me that Begetta had taken millions of our francs with him to Peru. I was beyond devastated. We were so happy and the business success had given us a perfect life. Now, without the business, it was all gone. I cried a lot during Christmas that year and Gabe spent many hours talking to people and trying to see how he could fix this catastrophe.

Within a few weeks of the stranger's call, however, our life began to change. First, the two cars were re-possessed and quickly after that we had to let go both Madeleine and the gardener. I can still hear Catherine's sobs when I told her Madeleine would no longer live with us. How do you explain losing a fortune to a seven year old?

Since declaring bankruptcy was considered a crime in France, Gabe could have gone to jail. So we had to come up with a large sum of money to pay all of his suppliers. That's when my mother came to our rescue and offered to sell Lerina so she could give me my share of the proceeds. Years earlier she had to put that house in her children's names to keep my father's creditors from taking it.

GABE

What happened in November 1954 was entirely my fault and I will regret it as long as I live. I should not have pursued the expansion of my business so quickly. I definitely should not have trusted a competitor like Roma, especially since I knew how cut throat he and his Grassois friends were. Most importantly, I should have hired a financial advisor.

Although I tried, I could not convince any of my suppliers to work with me. As far as they were concerned, I had committed to buy merchandise from them, and they were holding me to it.

Everyone in the industry knew Begetta had gone to Peru with all my money, but no one was willing to take a risk on me.

To add further insult, when a bankruptcy auction was held Roma told everyone in the industry that my perfume inventory was junk. Since no one else bid on it he was able to buy it at a deep discount.

Fortunately both the house and the factory buildings were still in my mother's name so they were not seized during these proceedings. Much of the antique furniture also was protected since it was in Claudine's name, through a prenuptial agreement protecting her assets. This was the only good outcome because we were able to remain in the house without fear of being evicted.

To make matters worse another one of my friendly competitors who claimed indebtedness to my father—this time for having set him up in business—persuaded me to apply for the French equivalent of bankruptcy, called "faillite." This guy offered to walk me through the process and to help me financially once the bankruptcy was completed. Once I declared bankruptcy, I never saw this person again. Again, I didn't check into this man's motives.

Although I had a marketable skill in perfumery, over the next two years I was rejected by every perfume house in France. I was willing to relocate to Grasse, Paris or anywhere else to stay in my profession. However, everyone I approached had an excuse for not hiring me. That's when I finally realized the extent of the Grassois perfumers' vendetta against me. The perfume business was all I knew. I had absolutely no other skills—I had never been capable of either building or fixing anything. Ultimately we were so desperate for money that I started washing cars in a garage in Golfe-Juan.

CLAUDINE

The work options were just as grim for me. I had never worked and always had household help so I couldn't even be hired out to cook or clean. I simply had never done it. Fortunately, Charles and Zaza came to our rescue. They hired me to pack products for shipping at their pottery factory in Vallauris.

It was all surreal. Overnight, I went from living almost "the life of the rich and famous" to working for our food. I was on my feet all day, next to the people making the pottery. The air was very dusty and it was so cold in the winter months my hands were always frozen. I was constantly afraid of dropping the pottery and breaking it; fearing I would get fired.

Since our jobs were certainly not paying enough for private school, we took the girls out of the Catholic school in Cannes and once again enrolled them at the public school in Golfe-Juan. Since there was no one at home during the day, their uncle Claude would walk down to the school and take them to my mother in law's apartment across from our house. At night, Gabe cooked a simple meal and we ate as a family—something we only did before during holidays or other special occasions. I had never learned to cook and had no interest in learning how. Since our social life had come to a very quick end, we spent nights at home trying to figure out to survive in light of Gabe's inability to regain his profession.

There was only one positive thing that happened during this awful period; my father Roger heard about the business failure and in July 1955 he invited us to spend some time at his farm outside of Paris, named Condé. It was a beautiful estate with several houses and even had farm animals like chickens and rabbits. The girls loved the farm and gave each animal a name. They also got to spend time with the grandfather they barely knew. It was wonderful for me too because he had changed so much—he was now the person I remembered before money ruined him. He was kind, patient and loving; something I credited to his new wife Yolande who placed a lot of value on family relationships.

Gabe and Claudine at Condé, July 1955

One day, the girls found a dead bird and decided it should be buried. So they identified a good burying spot and dug a little grave. Then they decided the dead bird would be lonely by itself so they dug additional graves to include other animals. When they ran out of animals before they had filled all the graves, they decided to include their grandfather in that cemetery—for later burial of course. At that point, he arrived on the scene and inquired about the cemetery. The girls told him he was included because he would be the best person to keep the animals company. This made him laugh and he told that story to many people.

This would be the last time I would see him; he died seven years later and I was not able to go to his funeral.

GABE

As it turned out, help came from an unexpected source. For years after the war, we had exchanged Christmas cards with Bill Yarborough, the American colonel I met in 1944 after the allies landed in Normandy. We had seen him again in 1954 when Bill came to France in June to celebrate the 10th anniversary of the Normandy landing.

We mailed very few Christmas cards in December 1954 but we did send one to Bill, telling him about the business failure. He wrote back immediately and invited me to the Army War College in Carlisle, Pennsylvania, where he was stationed. His letter was very encouraging because he thought there was a good chance I could find a perfumer's job in the states, especially in New York. Bill also said he would be our sponsor—a critical requirement for anyone who wanted to immigrate to the states prior to having a job.

Bill's willingness to sponsor us made the decision to immigrate possible. As a sponsor he would be financially responsible for us while we were in the states. If we got sick or ran out of money, he was on the hook. He also was vouching for our character and our ability to assimilate into the American culture and way of life.

We managed to scrape together enough money for a plane ticket so I could fly to Pennsylvania in early February 1955. I stayed with Bill and his family in Carlisle and he was kind enough to chauffeur me into New York City where I had an interview with a large perfume company. I thought the interview went rather well; a few days later they offered me a job. I was ecstatic, but soon the euphoria was shattered. Unfortunately, the company also had an office in Paris run by a close friend of one of my former competitors and they withdrew the job offer without giving me a reasonable excuse. It seemed the Grassois mafia was still committed to keeping me out of the perfume business, even beyond France. I flew back to France quickly after that, unable to schedule another interview.

In the end, the decision to go to America was made easier by factors other than having lost everything, almost overnight. Not only were we out of financial options, but several of our "intimate" friends also turned their backs on us. The social class structure was very well defined in France in the fifties. Once you lost your standing, especially if it involved a failed business, some people suddenly decided you were not worth their precious time.

For Claudine and me this was particularly painful because our lifestyle, our friends, and my success all mattered a great deal to us. I was mortified that I had been so careless, so arrogant and had lacked the necessary business skills to properly manage my affairs.

But the shame did not end there. The perfume mafia felt compelled to rub it in even more. The sordid affair really came to a head when some of my former competitors came to the garage where I was washing cars just to laugh at me. That's when I knew I could never again be a perfumer in France.

By December 1955 we were facing another difficult Christmas and that's when we decided to leave France for America. This was a difficult decision because we knew the girls would not be able to come with us. I would have to find a job first.

New Year's Eve celebration in Cannes, December 1955.
Left to right: Zaza, Charles, Claudine, Gabe, Charlotte
and Roger (two months before leaving for America).

Leaving France was a great leap into the unknown. We knew virtually no one in America. I didn't have a job there and we had very little money. Also, Claudine didn't speak any English and she had always been very close to her mother and Zaza. Family was everything to her.

After the bankruptcy, we focused on earning enough money to cover our daily living expenses. Washing cars and packing pottery was barely enough. Claudine received money from her mother, when Charlotte sold her house in Golfe-Juan. That allowed us to pay off most of our creditors and it kept me out of prison. It also supplemented our meager earnings so that we could buy two one way tickets by ship to New York on the Andrea Doria.

CHAPTER 9

FAILURE WAS NOT AN OPTION

CLAUDINE

In addition to saving enough money for the trip to America, Gabe and I also had to find someone to take care of our daughters until we could send for them. Fortunately, Zaza and Charles offered to take them as long as necessary. This way the girls could stay in the Golfe-Juan public school, which was important since they already had experienced so many changes in their lives.

Before we decided both of us would go to America, I briefly considered staying in France with the girls. After all, they were only eight and nine years old. My mother Charlotte did not believe men could remain faithful when separated from their wives so she urged me to go with Gabe. Admittedly, she had years of experience with my father's infidelities so she was a bit jaded.

My father Roger had never been a fan of Gabe's. He considered him a playboy with no business sense, so he begged me to divorce him and stay in France. He even offered to support me and the girls, anything to keep me in France. In the end, I decided to go to America because I loved Gabe and I wanted to be with him when we made this dramatic change in our lives.

We had no idea how long it would be for Gabe to find a job,

but in spite of what had taken place in France, I really hoped that it would be different in America. I thought we would finally catch a break.

The day before we left, we moved the girls' beds and dresser to Charles and Zaza's house, along with all of their clothes and toys. Marie-Anne had an awful ear ache and was clinging to me for comfort. That night we went out to dinner with some friends.

When I think back to that time, I find it very odd that we spent our last night in France having dinner with friends rather than staying home with the girls. Everything was abnormal then, including some of the decisions we made. It's impossible to describe the heartache of leaving young children behind. You have to live through a similar situation to understand. The girls were simply too young to know what had taken place, why we had to leave and why we couldn't take them with us. We wanted to protect them from the truth. Nevertheless, I was afraid they would feel abandoned, much the same way I had felt when my father had left us when I was young.

When we woke up on February 2, the ground was covered with a light snow stunning all of us. My mother and her new husband (also unfortunately named Roger, along with the last name of Villain!) arrived before lunch, very upset by the weather and all of the accidents on the road. We waited for Gabe to arrive so we could have lunch, thinking he was running late due to the bad roads. When he finally arrived with his arm in a sling, I got hysterical and started yelling it was an omen and we shouldn't go. When Gabe reminded me that our one way tickets were non-refundable, I realized I had to calm down.

As much as the unexpected snow and Gabe's dislocated shoulder put additional stress on an already tough situation, it also kept us from focusing on the heartbreak of leaving the girls. Somehow we managed to eat lunch, finished packing and soon it was time to go to the harbor in Cannes.

It's hard to think back to that time without getting very

emotional. The girls were clinging to us, refusing to let us go. Everyone was crying, knowing there was nothing that could be done about this situation. We had to leave them behind at the house with Zaza and Charles' maid. I would continue to see their faces many years later, crying and begging us not to go,

GABE

Because of the snow only a very small group of loyal friends were waiting to see Claudine and I board the Andrea Doria at the port of Cannes. There were a lot of tears, hugs and good luck words exchanged but many of these friends thought we were crazy to be doing this. In the fifties, it was inconceivable for most people who lived in Europe and had established life styles and connections to even consider moving to another country. It was simply just too risky. The only person who favored this giant leap was my mother-in-law Charlotte. She understood there was no future for me in France and she believed America would provide the only chance for me to regain my profession.

Everyone else told us not to go, especially since I had gone to America in 1955 and was not able to secure a perfume job. They were telling me to stay in France and start another career as a traveling salesman. I wondered if they just wanted to keep us in France because they enjoyed our company or if they might be right.

There was no way to put a positive spin on this decision. We were facing enormous challenges and were going blind into a foreign country, without a job waiting for me. In those days, the US government welcomed immigrants but you were on your own. If you didn't have a job lined up first, you had to have a sponsor—and that person took on a tremendous responsibility. Once you arrived, the sponsor was financially responsible for you. If you didn't find work quickly or became ill or ran out of money, your sponsor was expected to take care of you. We lucked out when Bill Yarborough offered to sponsor us. Had he not offered, we never would have gone because no one else who would have taken a chance on us.

CLAUDINE

In addition to our one way tickets, a steamer trunk and several pieces of luggage, Gabe and I only had $600 in cash and a tourist visa that did not allow either of us to work in America. Also, other than Bill Yarborough in Pennsylvania, we only knew two other people living in America at that time—a French couple related to one of our friends, who worked for the United Nations.

At the pier we went through the formalities, checking our bags and then saying goodbye to family and friends. We were all so emotional that in the confusion I totally forgot to hug Zaza goodbye! My poor aunt was so upset with me she left the pier crying and screaming about how selfish I was. I ran after her and kissed her goodbye right before the launch left the pier to take us to the ship.

As you can imagine, I was totally drained and exhausted. Between leaving my two young girls, my entire family and our friends, Gabe's accident and the snow, I was in a state of total confusion.

I kept thinking: what if we go through all of this and still Gabe doesn't find a job? What then? Do we go back to France, and then what? After his unsuccessful trip to America in 1955, we decided to look into immigrating to Canada. Gabe, the girls and I took a train to Paris to apply for a Visa at the Canadian embassy. After a day of going from one office to another and filling out endless forms, we were rejected. Since my grandmother Rachel was a prominent member of the Socialist Party in France we were considered undesirable in Canada. So America was our only chance.

It took nine days to cross the Atlantic on the Andrea Doria and we had bad storms during the entire journey—a difficult combination of very cold wind and rain, so strong we could never go up on deck for some fresh air. Since we had third class tickets, we were in the bottom third of the boat along with many other immigrants whose financial situations were similar to ours. Soon most passengers were seasick and no amount of scrubbing could erase the stench of vomit.

The sea was so rough passengers had to be escorted to and from their staterooms. Soon that became problematic problematic so the staff strung ropes between posts so that passengers could go into the dining room. Fortunately, we had spent enough time on yachts we were not affected by the rolling ship. Eventually, Gabe and I along with two elderly American women were the only passengers in the deserted dining room. Gabe was in constant pain from his dislocated shoulder and could not use his arm so I cut his food for him. The staff finally felt so sorry for us and those two women they allowed us to dine in the second class dining room, where the odor of sea sick passengers was less offensive. Since our fellow 3rd class passengers, mostly Italians, were all throwing up, they were refused access to that dining room and were sent away with only oranges. It was really heartbreaking.

GABE

As bad as the trip was, especially with my still throbbing shoulder, at least the ship brought us to America safely. Barely five months later on July 26, the Andrea Doria collided with the MS Stockholm off the coast of Nantucket in Massachusetts. It sank 11 hours after being struck and 46 people lost their lives. After months of research it was determined that heavy fog, coupled with high speeds in poor visibility and using radar incorrectly contributed to the collision. The accident remains today the worst maritime disaster in United States waters since the sinking of the SS Eastland in 1915.

So we were very lucky to have left in February rather than that fateful day in July. After all the bad luck we had during the past two years, at least we were spared a ship wreck and we were grateful for that.

Exhausted from the trip, we arrived in New York on a bitterly cold February 11. I will always remember coming into New York harbor and seeing the Statue of Liberty. It wasn't just because France had given that statue to America; it was truly a sign that we were welcomed to a country that would treat us better than the one we had just left behind. I understood, nevertheless, that Lady Liberty offered us a chance at success, but not a guarantee.

Since the ship held more than one thousand passengers and crew, the debarkation took hours and Claudine kept saying she was glad to have her mink coat for warmth. I can assure you she was the only passenger coming out of third class with that kind of coat.

Bill Yarborough had made a reservation for us at the Picadilly Hotel on West 45th Street near Times Square and he was there to greet us. We had dinner together in the hotel and then he left us to so we could get settled in. We both fell into the first sound sleep we'd had in months.

Since Bill didn't know how bad our financial situation was, he had booked us into a very nice hotel. Although we would have loved to have stayed there, our $600 would not have lasted long. So we moved uptown to the Cameron Hotel on West 86th Street the next day. The Cameron accommodations included a very small kitchenette with a hot plate, a toaster and a tiny refrigerator. This allowed us to save money by cooking meals. We had our first supermarket shopping experience where we bought $8 dollars' worth of food and accessories. Soon even that hotel was too expensive and we moved again even further uptown to the Whitehall Hotel on West 100th Street where we created a bit of a sensation as the only white residents. Clearly this was worlds away from the Villa D'Este.

Eventually we found a tiny furnished apartment in the basement of a building at 48 West 75th Street, which did not have a private bathroom. Sharing a bathroom with strangers was common in Europe, but it had not been something we had ever done. Claudine refused to cross the hall in a bathrobe and insisted on being fully dressed instead, in case anyone was lining up for the bathroom.

The building's owner was a Jewish doctor who had a rather unusual clientele of black women who came late in the day. We suspected he might be an abortionist.

CLAUDINE

Although our tourist visas did not allow Gabe and me to work, we knew our $600 was not going to last us very long. So we asked our French friends who worked at the United Nations if they knew of any jobs we could have without getting in trouble with the authorities. Through this connection, I became a nanny for a French couple who also worked at the UN. They were very pleased to find someone who spoke French so their children could learn the language.

As you'll recall, our nanny Nounou took care of the girls when they were little. Now I was taking care of someone else's young children and I had to pretend I knew what I was doing. I had to learn fast. The children were two years and fifteen months old and I had them from 9 in the morning until 6 at night. This was many years before Pampers, so I also had to wash their cloth diapers in the bath tub since there was no washing machine or diaper service.

You might think I'm exaggerating but this is the God's honest truth. I had to walk 35 blocks to my employers' apartment on Riverside Drive wearing my alligator heels since I didn't own a pair of sensible shoes. As you can imagine, my feet were in agony each day as I walked to work. I also continued to wear my five carat diamond ring and gold watch, which was a very bad idea in New York, especially walking alone so many blocks. I figured eventually I would have to sell both pieces and I wanted to wear them as long as possible. It was foolish of me to hold on to these things but I really needed them to remember my former life.

That job only paid $15 a week but they gave me lunch every day. I had become so frugal that I saved half of my sandwich and an apple that I brought home for Gabe since he most likely wouldn't eat anything all day.

Every night Gabe would fix a very simple dinner in our tiny apartment. Eating was always a challenge because we didn't have a table and chairs. We would eat either sitting on a suitcase or on the bed with the plates on our laps. The bed only had three legs so it was always tilting to one side and often our plates would end up on the floor, depending on which side of the bed you sat on. This was definitely light years from the environment we had at Juliette-Antoinette in Golfe-Juan.

GABE

While Claudine was spending her days as a nanny, I was walking dozens of blocks in Manhattan looking for work and also spending time in phone booths calling fragrance houses. In early March, I received a letter from Procter and Gamble asking me to come to Cincinnati for an interview. We were ecstatic and even dared to dream about a potential job offer.

Before I had a chance to present myself to P&G, the Grassois mafia got to work again. I learned that the French office of P&G had contacted people in Grasse to ask about me and the interview was cancelled. Through an acquaintance I found out I was being barred from the profession, even overseas. For me, that was the lowest point so far in this whole sordid tale.

We began to fear we might be forced to go home, and yet by then we didn't have enough money for the return passage.

Luck finally struck when I was able to get an interview with Shulton (maker of Old Spice). Even though they didn't have a perfumer's position at the time, the VP of Personnel asked to see my resume. I had no idea what a resume was since I had never used one. This VP was so stunned anyone would look for work without a resume that he started writing one for me. A few days later he sent me some copies, which I began to use to secure interviews.

For me that VP became the essence of what America was all about—people who were willing to help you get ahead. There were tremendous opportunities in this country, when you looked for it.

The memory that has always stayed with me, however, about our first year in America is the day in April when I stood on a corner in Manhattan and inserted a dime into the pay phone. With my new resume, I had interviewed at Felton, a Brooklyn-based perfume company, and I hoped to get good news. They offered me a job, starting the following Monday, paying me $93 per week.

This was a miracle. We were down to our last $2.00 and we thought our only option was repatriation by going to the French Embassy. Until I got my first pay check, we borrowed

$100 from our UN French friends. With that first pay check, we bought an iron and a clock radio. We have kept that radio in our bedroom for decades as a reminder.

As grateful as we were for the opportunity at Felton, we had always hoped to end up in a small town. Since I had never lived in a large city and Claudine hadn't lived in one since 1939, we were not big city people and we wanted to live in a small town. I started sending my resume out to quite of few fragrance houses outside of New York. One of our challenges was lacking a phone in our apartment so on my resume I used the number of Claudine's employer.

We didn't know that the Shulton VP of Personnel had forwarded my resume to their research director who was a personal friend of Bernard Polak, who founded Polak's Frutal Works (PFW), a fragrance company in Middletown, NY, a small city in Orange County about fifty miles from Manhattan.

One night in early June Claudine was just about to leave her nanny position when she received a call came from Bernard Polak. He said he was in town and wanted to know if we could have dinner with him the following night. Claudine, who was excited to hear this and eager to make a good impression, told Bernard we would be very happy to meet with him. He suggested having dinner at the Sheraton Park, which was at 56th and Broadway but Claudine, not knowing English well, thought he had said the Sheraton Hotel at Park Avenue.

The taxis were on strike that day, so we ran to make this appointment only to learn we had the wrong address. As a result we arrived at the Sheraton Park more than an hour late, disheveled and sweaty from running. Bernard was very gracious when we explained our lateness and we settled in to a wonderful dinner and a very productive meeting.

One week later, I received an offer from Polak's Frutal Works, paying me $8,500 a year. I would be their first French perfumer, and I would eventually become their chief perfumer.

CHAPTER 10

THE PLANE IS ON FIRE; SAVE YOURSELF!

CATHERINE

Our parents were gone on a ship to America. Why? And why didn't they take us with them? When we asked why they had to leave, all we were told was "they had to; they had no choice." So we were now living with our great aunt Zaza and great uncle Charles at L'Oustalet in Golfe-Juan. They did everything they could to cheer us up, but nothing worked for Marie-Anne. She cried almost all the time; once she cried so long she got the hiccups and they wouldn't go away. Zaza and Charles kept telling us things would be fine, that they loved us and were thrilled we were with them.

We were trying to understand why our lives had changed so much when everything was perfect. We weren't told about the mess with the perfume business, and we didn't know Doddy had tried but could not find a job in his field. We knew Mounette went to work with Zaza and Charles but we were never told Doddy was washing cars. I doubt we would have believed it. Since we were sheltered from these details, especially losing all of their money, we couldn't understand why they had left us behind. We didn't know they only had enough money for two tickets on that ship. We also didn't think about where the money would come from. There had always been money in France so we just didn't understand how Doddy couldn't find money in America.

Since we were so young everyone thought it best to shield us from the truth. Eventually we stopped asking why they left. We just wanted to know when we would see them again, but that was a question no one could answer.

Zaza and Charles were an interesting couple. He was tall and domineering due to his height, but he was a softie. He loved to play tricks on people (and kids) and to make us laugh. Unfortunately he sometimes chose the wrong time to make people laugh—like when he came to see me in the hospital after I had my appendix out. I must have been around six and although I kept telling him to stop making me laugh as that made my side hurt, he kept right on telling me his funny stories. He had the bluest eyes and they twinkled when he smiled. I never heard him say a bad word about anyone. Whenever he spoke about or looked at Zaza, it was obvious he adored her.

Zaza was always smiling or laughing and she loved to eat. Since she was rather short and tended to be on the chunky side, she was always on a diet. When her maid Alfreda served dessert, she always pushed it away, insisting she was "aux regime" (on a diet) but before the table was cleared she always helped herself to a bit of sweet. As hard as she tried, she did not lose weight. Her girth was a source of frustration all of her life; especially since her sister Charlotte, my grandmother, was always thin. Like Marie-Anne, Charlotte was sickly as a child and her liver was compromised. As a result she often complained of "une crise de foie" (a liver crisis) that made her nauseous.

Zaza and Charles were very much in love. Their greatest source of sadness was to learn they would never be able to have children, after multiple miscarriages. Instead, they made their ceramic business their child and worked it successfully for many years.

They also loved sex, but this I learned much later in life. Mounette, who worked in their pottery factory for a couple of years, told me they had a special hand signal to indicate when one of them wanted to have sex. They would meet in a closet in the back of the factory where they had some kind of bed. Based on what Mounette told me, this happened quite frequently.

Mounette would write every week; one letter was addressed to Marie-Anne and me and the other one to Zaza. In our letter she mostly wrote about all the new things they were experiencing; how big New York city was, how fast people talked, how they were always in a hurry, and how often she made mistakes when she spoke English. One of her biggest challenges was mastering the "th" sound when it came before a consonance—as in the word "thruway" which she could only pronounce as "truway."

In one of Mounette's letters we learned that one day, as she was walking on the street in Manhattan, a bus stopped and a woman yelled out "Claudine!" and it turned out to be Marina Kobzef, her best school friend in Paris. Marina was Russian and she and her husband Ygor had come to America years ago and that's when she and Mounette had lost touch. Here she was on the street in Manhattan and she had seen Mounette from the bus! What were the odds? Marie-Anne and I had never met Marina but we were glad Mounette had reconnected with her and that she now had a friend in America.

Yet even though Mounette's letters sounded like they were happy in America, something told me Zaza was getting a different story. Once I saw her crying as she was reading Mounette's letter. Also when Mamie Charlotte came to visit us she didn't mention anything about what was happening in America. That made me wonder if our parents weren't happy there.

We stayed at L'Oustalet through the school year and then moved to Le Pin Pignou in the hills of Vallauris for the summer.

This property was pure magic for a child. There was a very large two story stucco home surrounded by many acres of land that local farmers would rent from my great aunt and great uncle. During that summer we walked around and helped ourselves to figs, artichokes, and strawberries or we went through rows and rows of glorious and sweet smelling roses. I later learned many of the farmers who rented Zaza and Charles' land were growing roses for the same perfumers who drove our parents out of France.

For years I thought our time with Charles and Zaza lasted a couple of years because as an eight year old, it seemed a long time. Yet, I only have tidbits of recollections about that time in our lives. One of them is of their maid Alfreda in the kitchen at Le Pin Pignou, helping her pluck feathers from a chicken she had just slaughtered. I went to the chicken house daily to gather eggs but I only went with her once to watch her wring that poor chicken's neck so we could enjoy it for dinner. Eating a fresh chicken is nothing like one you buy in a supermarket. It has an incredible taste—so delectable in fact that a just killed chicken was considered the best meat to serve company; much better than beef.

During that summer Charles hired a tutor for us, so we could learn enough English to get by once we got to America. All I recall from these weekly tutoring sessions is that Marie-Anne and I made fun of each other as we mispronounced words. After a while, the tutor was sent away.

Also during the summer of 1956, Zaza and Charles sent us for a couple of weeks to Valberg, a mountainous village just one hour from Golfe-Juan with our grandmother Juliette and our aunt Marcelle. I wondered if it was also to take us out of the salt air as Mounette once told me. Chances are it was mostly because it became difficult for Alfreda to continue her maid duties and also be responsible for us. In any case, this was not at all the same type of vacation I remembered with Nounou when we went to Italy. There were lots of rules with my grandmother and aunt, and there were frequent visits to the local church. The only activity that pleased my sister and me was the daily "goûter" or tea which included fancy pastries from the shop down the street.

The summer passed quickly and we returned to L'Oustalet to start school. By October we still did not know when we would be joining our parents in New York. We knew from Mounette's letters that Doddy had gotten a job in April, so why were we still in France?

We finally learned our parents had been trying for months to secure our Visas but they kept getting the run-around from the immigration services. Since it now appeared we would be in France longer than expected, Zaza and Charles even considered buying a pony for us.

Finally in early November our visas came in Mounette's letter! She wrote that their friend Bill Yarbrough had come through once more. Since their efforts had been unsuccessful, they reached out to Bill for help. He suggested they write to their congresswoman Katherine Saint-George and she helped them get the right forms for our visas.

Zaza and Charles only had a few weeks to get used to the idea that we were leaving and to prepare us for our flight. We needed different clothes for the New York climate. Since we had always lived on the French Riviera, we didn't even have a proper coat. Zaza took us shopping and the first items she bought were red wool duffel coats—the kind with the wooden buttons that tied with rope. We also got winter shoes and sweaters and pants. It all seemed so strange compared to the clothes we had always worn.

Our plane tickets arrived and that's when we learned we would be leaving on November 23. We had little time to pack and even less time to say goodbye to our family and our school friends. I don't remember much of this but I suspect there were lots of tears.

Our plane was scheduled to leave from the Nice airport, fly

to Barcelona, then on to Lisbon and finally stop in the Azores for re-fueling before heading toward America. Zaza and Charles were very worried about us flying alone but there were no other options. They had a business to run and could not take the time off. Mamie Charlotte also could not make the trip with us; I don't believe she had ever flown before.

When we got to the airport in Nice, a very nice stewardess reassured us that she would watch over us carefully. In addition, there was a young American couple on the flight who spoke French and they agreed to look out for us as well.

In keeping with our parents' trip to New York, we also were plagued by the weather. The winds were so fierce we had to spend the night in the Azores, rather than just stop there to refuel. We were taken to a hotel at the airport where we had dinner, and that nice American couple who spoke French stayed with us the whole time. They were so nice they even made sure we got into our pajamas, brushed our teeth and then they tucked us in bed.

CLAUDINE

When those visas finally arrived, Gabe and I were ecstatic. In fact, we even bought a bottle of French wine to celebrate! We were finally going to get our girls back after all these months.

Of course I was terrified of that plane ride! They were so young and only spoke French and they were used to always having an adult with them. How would they be able to handle this alone? There were also three different stops before they would even land at Idlewild Airport in Queens. What if they got lost somehow? I was a nervous wreck the whole week before they were going to travel.

November 23 arrived and Gabe and I were on our way to

the airport. All during the ride I was thinking of the "what ifs?" and I said to him:

"What happens when a plane crashes? What do they tell the people waiting for the passengers?"

He says to me:

"Oh, they probably initially tell them that the plane is delayed."

Sure enough, we get to the airport and we learn their plane is delayed! I got hysterical and Gabe had to calm me down.

We ended up waiting nearly 24 hours for that plane to land. Every time we asked for an update, all we were told was: "There is no more information Madame. The plane is delayed."

CATHERINE

It was a long trip but finally we were about to land. Marie-Anne, who had been scared out of her mind the entire trip, had finally fallen into a sound sleep. I was shaking her, trying to get her to wake up and look out the window to see the tall buildings of New York.

"Alors, Marie-Anne, réveille-toi. Tu manque tous!" (Marie-Anne, wake up. You're missing everything!")

She still wouldn't wake up so I shouted in her ear: "L'avion est en feu!" Sauve toi!" ("The plane is on fire; save yourself.")

That got her attention and she woke up with a start and started screaming. Then she slapped me right across the face but when she realized there was no fire, she calmed down. She apologized for slapping me and then, finally, she looked out the window and saw New York below.

Soon we were in our parents' arms and with that the ten months of separation were almost forgotten. They kept telling us how much we had changed (in 10 months?) and how grown up we looked. Mounette kept apologizing for having left us.

"If I had any idea we would be separated for 10 long months, I never would have left you," she kept saying.

We were happy to see Doddy no longer had his arm in a sling so he could hug us again like before. Mounette was still the same; she talked non-stop and kept kissing us. While we were waiting for our luggage, we tried to take in as much as we could. We were amazed at the size of the airport, how many people were there and how New Yorkers dressed so differently. We had heard in France how much Americans loved cheeseburgers and so we wanted one. Then we asked for American ice cream. That day, we decided there is no better dessert than American ice cream. We pretty much got whatever we wanted at the airport.

Eventually, we were in the car headed for home to New Hampton, NY. When Doddy got the job at Polak's in Middletown, NY, they moved out of Manhattan and rented a house in New Hampton, about 10 miles from Middletown.

Marie-Anne and I were mesmerized by the bridges, the tall city buildings, the highways and how fast the cars traveled. There was no snow on the ground that day but it was very cold. I recall the ride from the airport to New Hampton took forever but it was actually well under two hours.

We really didn't know what to expect. Mounette kept saying the house was very different from anything we had ever lived in before, but that it was comfortable and we could each have our own bedroom. But since we had always shared, we chose to continue doing so. That made Mounette very happy since she had just learned (but would not tell us for another month) that she was pregnant and the baby was due early July 1957.

CHAPTER 11

AS AMERICAN AS APPLE PIE

CATHERINE

When Doddy started working at Polak's Frutal Works in June 1956, he was not earning enough money to live in Middletown, New York, where the company was located. So he and Mom had rented a house in New Hampton, a small hamlet in Orange County just outside of Middletown. Its only claim to fame was that it was near Pine Island where "rich black dirt" allowed this town to grow the most pungent onion, some 30,000 pounds per acre. The "sweet" scent reached us in New Hampton.

The house in New Hampton, a farming community about two hours from Manhattan, was a small ranch. Since we had never seen a single story house in France, it was a different dwelling for us and could have fit in one half of a floor at Juliette- Antoinette. It was the first house in a small development, surrounded by farms.

A breezeway led to either the house on the left or the one car garage on the right. A side door let you into the kitchen large enough to accommodate a washing machine and a dryer. The rectangular-shaped living room had picture windows looking out to the street, and a small dining area was off to one side.

Three small bedrooms and one bathroom occupied the back of the house.

There was also a large basement—something else we had never seen in France. It came in handy the following summer because it was the coolest room in the house; there was no air conditioning. As far as we were concerned, it was very different from what we were used to but it was perfect because we were together again.

We arrived two days before Thanksgiving and the very next week Marie-Anne and I started school at Saint John's Catholic in Goshen. Our parents said we had to learn English quickly so that we could do well in school. We were thrilled to ride the yellow school bus; something else new for us. Our first day of school was surreal as the word quickly spread about the two French girls. Some of the students treated us like celebrities while others thought of us as fodder for pranks. Since we didn't speak any English we didn't know who was being kind and who was making fun of us.

As much as our parents wanted us to learn English quickly, they also wanted us to retain our French. They insisted that we continue speaking French at home. Although this was a laudable goal, it made learning English quickly a bit tough since it was limited to when school was in session. Although I complained about how unfair that was, years later I admitted that being bilingual looked good on a resume.

In any case, that first day of school, I was going through the lunch line and an attendant gave me a carton of milk. I had never acquired a taste for milk after infancy so I shook my head no and said:

"Du vin, s'il vous plait." (Some win, please)

There was a logical reason for my request. French kids were given wine mixed with water at a very young age because it was considered good for the digestion. Naturally, the cafeteria attendant didn't know what I was saying so she called for Mr.

Cohen, the French teacher. When he translated my request, they all started laughing at me and he explained that American schools never served wine.

"Mr. Cohen was very nice to you and Marie-Anne," Mounette said. "I called him often during those early months because you and Marie-Anne weren't speaking English as quickly as we had hoped. He told me that it would take at least three months while you mostly listened to others, and then you would start to speak English."

Mr. Cohen was a smart man. Right after Easter, Marie-Anne and I came home from school and we were speaking English to each other. We had spent four months listening carefully to the correct pronunciation before we felt comfortable enough to speak. From that day forward we never spoke to each other in French again; we were that determined to become Americans. Also, I decided that the name Cathy was more American than Catherine so I told everyone I was Cathy from then on. Soon after that, Doddy and Mounette were re-named Dad and Mom, to further accentuate our new life. I even tried to acquire a taste for milk but that failed.

We lived in New Hampton until June 1958 and Marie-Anne and I used that time to finalize our roadmap to full-blooded Americans. The previous December we had taken part in a Christmas pageant using hula hoops to dance to the song "Winter Wonderland". We were still in Catholic school and the nuns told us we had to keep that hoop around our waists, without swaying our hips too provocatively! Try that sometimes.

I had fallen in love with Elvis and always wore a small metal pin with his picture. I took it off at night and kept it on my night table to I would be sure to wear it again the next day. We joined after school clubs and started spending time with neighborhood kids. I even had a "boyfriend" within a year—Vinnie Sonak— who lived on the farm you could see from our house. The Sonaks had a pond where Marie-Anne and I learned to ice skate.

During the winter of 1957 Vinnie's mother passed away and he started missing a lot of school; his grades took a dive. I will always remember how Sister Mary-Vincent treated him when he returned to school. She made him stand up in front of the whole class as she told all of us how awful his grades were. From that day on, I started questioning the value of a Catholic education.

Also about this time I started challenging my parents' child rearing techniques. Since Marie-Anne and I had spent much of our childhood in France with either Nounou or Madeleine, I had not yet experienced their "disappointments toward inappropriate behavior." Now that they were in charge, I started getting punished a lot. The more I questioned their rules, the more I realized growing older was not easy in our house.

"Just wait until your father gets home," Mom said to me often. I didn't understand why she couldn't just dictate the punishment. Why was he always the bad guy? In reality, I was far more terrified of her because he was the one with the soft touch.

Dad did not believe in physical punishment so instead he devised a rather archaic way of teaching me better behavior. He wanted me to learn French history. So whenever I stepped out of line, which was often, he directed me to copy pages from his many books, especially the French Revolution. In addition to teaching me about this historic event, my father's strategy was also to preserve my French.

"Catherine — 40 pages," I would hear as often as "Wait until your father gets home." I was constantly measured against Marie-Anne who never did anything wrong. But no matter how often I got punished, I kept asking why there were so many restrictions on my life. Why was I kept from having fun? By the time I left home for college, I had copied much of Dad's three volume set of French history books. I retained, however, very few facts about the French revolution other than lots of royals lost their head and a guy named Robespierre was a terror.

Admittedly, my belligerence came at a bad time. Mom

was having a tough time. She was impatiently waiting for her pregnancy to end, still trying to adapt to her new life without staff, and learning the language. Fortunately her neighbor Dotty Dombrosky, who was also raising children about our age, took pity on her. Dotty helped her learn more English, and taught her to pronounce words more accurately. She failed, however, to have her master that "th" sound before a consonant. Dotty was even kind enough to give Mom some of her recipes so she might decide to cook for us.

That last attempt didn't work out very well so Dad continued cooking dinner. His approach was to cook various meats all together on Sunday night— chicken, pork, and beef— and then reheat everything during the week. The dinners were predictable and tasteless—they always started with Campbell's soup, followed by a reheated meat (all tasting the same since they had cooked together and for the same length of time), a frozen vegetable and ice cream for dessert. We were seated promptly at 6 PM and we inhaled the food. Within twenty minutes, we were finished, the table was cleared and the dishes done and put away. I asked Mom why she didn't cook since she had more time at home than Dad.

"My mother never cooked because we always had servants who did the cooking so, to me, it was not something I should learn to do," Mom explained. And that was that.

I still found it odd that they had such wonderful meals cooked for them in France and yet they now settled for this awful food. I stopped asking about this since I was already questioning too many aspects of my new American life. I could tell Mom was getting frustrated by my probing questions.

Our kind neighbor Dotty also helped me with a school fund raising project. I had signed up to sell religious paint by number drawings and since I didn't know many people in our community, Dotty introduced me to them, told them I was from France and wanted to help my school. Our neighbors lived quite a distance away so Dotty had to drive me all around. The net result was I sold enough of these drawings to get a prize. Although I could have chosen anything from jewelry to dolls, I chose an archery set. Dad set up the target in the front yard and I spent hours practicing my skill. I never really mastered archery, but during all those practice hours I stayed out of trouble which means I didn't get punished.

This doesn't apply to the time Marie-Anne and I were building "grass skirts" with some kids from the neighborhood. We were using large leaves connected with toothpicks to form long strands, which were then attached with string at the waist. My leaves were smaller than others and one of the kids told me I was using poison ivy and that it was bad for me. I had no idea what that was since we didn't have it in France, so I said "no it's not" and I rubbed the leaves all over my face. Two days later, I couldn't open my eyes and Mom had to take me to the doctor for a shot. It was one of the many times she told me I was punished for being stupid. I was in agony for weeks and I did learn from this experience. From that point on, I stayed away from poison ivy.

But the biggest excitement when we lived in New Hampton was the day our brother Steve was born. Mom was due on July 4 and she desperately wanted her American child born on that day. She missed it by four hours but several days later she came home with a healthy American baby boy. Marie-Anne and I were in heaven and for the rest of that summer Mom had plenty of help with the feeding, diapering and soothing of our new family member.

Our brother Steve Eric Raphel one day would become a fourth-generation perfumer, starting in the business at Felton in Brooklyn, where Dad first got a job. It's a small world indeed.

Dad had been at Polak'sFrutal Works for a year but the ladies who worked there still considered him an "odd celebrity ". From his first day on the job, he wore beautiful white leather beach slippers so they started calling him "the barefoot perfumer." He also worked with the traditional "perfumer's organ" which is a semi-circular desk with a sort of bookcase around the perimeter to store various small bottles of scents. Every afternoon prior to leaving for the day, he would remind the women in the office to "be sure to clean my organ."

"I was not yet aware the word organ had a totally different meaning," he told me. "So I didn't understand why this simple statement would cause them all to laugh hysterically."

His French ways were also a topic of conversation in the office. One day, he told me, a European salesman came to visit bringing his beautiful wife along.

"When I was introduced to his wife, I kissed her hand the European way," he said. "This totally shocked the ladies in the lab. They were certain her husband was going to punch me in the face."

He told me his co-workers often asked him about his life in France and he was very willing to talk to them about certain aspects of his former life. However, as soon as anyone asked what made him decide to come to America, he would end the conversation by saying "Oh, that's a long and boring story." I suspect some of them learned about the bankruptcy through their contacts in the business but they never mentioned it to him. What was most important to him was that he was liked and respected by all of his co-workers at Polak's. He knew he could trust them too.

CHAPTER 12

ONLY THE DOG SURVIVED

CATHERINE

In 1959 when Steve was two years old Dad decided we had outgrown the little house in New Hampton and we should move to a bigger house in Middletown. His salary had increased and he was also getting Christmas bonuses. He thought living in town, in a larger home, would be expected of PFW's chief perfumer.

The perfect house turned up on Mountain Avenue. It too was a ranch but twice as big as the one in New Hampton. It had an unusual flat roof and central air conditioning, which was rare in those days. Although it only had three bedrooms, they were much bigger than the ones in New Hampton, and most importantly there were two and a half bathrooms. The living room was grand and on one side featured large picture windows looking out to the back yard. In addition to the formal living room, there was a TV room and a laundry room. The kitchen was a good size and had a dining room parallel to it, with a pass-through window. It was a very modern house, totally unlike Juliette-Antoinette, but it was the biggest one on the street and that was important to my parents.

Of equal importance was that Polak's was financing the

purchase with no money down and a good interest rate; the monthly nut was just $90, excluding taxes.

One of the home's best features was the substantial backyard that had a flagstone patio that spread the length of the living room, with a garden extension alongside the master bedroom. In addition to the patio, which was built on top of a hill, the backyard included a perfect spot for a future swimming pool. Although there were neighbors on both sides, the backyard was rather private due to the deep slope beyond the grassy area that was a sort of "no man's land" and lush with trees. Downtown was a short ride from Mountain Avenue, so the house was very well situated.

The location of the house was critical for Dad because he could come home for lunch. He was, among many things, a creature of habit. By living in town he left the house at ten minutes to eight and was at work by eight. He went home for lunch at noon and was back in his office at one o'clock. The commute had him home by 5:10 each night. Keeping to a schedule was very important to Dad.

The only drawback to the address, as far as our parents were concerned, was that it was less than two miles from our school so we didn't qualify for the school bus. So Dad got the morning shift since Mom was busy with Steve, but she picked us up in the afternoon. This worked out well initially but as we got older and started having activities after school, this put a strain on Mom's end of the bargain. If the weather was good, we were expected to walk home.

To further complicate things, Dad came home one day with a silver blue Jaguar XKE convertible—a two-seater. Needless to say, Mom was shocked that he hadn't bothered to tell her he was going to buy this car. It was also a problem for us because now Marie-Anne had to sit on my lap, which was surely against the law. During the warm months Dad took the top down so we would get to school with hairstyles dictated by hurricane-strength winds.

In spite of the wind-blown hair and uncomfortable ride to school in the morning, moving to Middletown had many highlights—not the least of which was trading the pungent onion odor from New Hampton to the constantly-changing fruity scent that came from Polak's Frutal Works. The company had always been Middletown's air wick since its flavors division often added to its palette. Dad's division, the fragrance side, was not nearly as evident to the Middletownians' noses.

Marie-Anne and I were very excited about living in town in a much bigger house and even though we still had to share a bedroom we only had to share a bathroom with Steve. We moved in at the end of July and quickly got to know some of the neighborhood kids. That fall, we started 6th grade in a new Junior High school and since we were now fluent in English the adjustment was much easier than when we first arrived in America.

For reasons that were not explained to us, we were enrolled in Middletown's public school although there was a Catholic school in town. I think it might have had something to do with the lice scare at St. John's in Goshen—which was initially blamed on us since we were foreigners. Mom had several meetings with the principal to convince him we had never had lice in France, but that we were now living in a farming community which could be the source of the lice. Evidently, he was not persuaded and that soured Mom and Dad against Catholic schools.

The year after we moved into the house Dad's salary was increased again, and that allowed him to ship from France several pieces of antiques that had stayed in Juliette-Antoinette. His mother was selling the house and the antiques would have become part of the sale if he didn't claim them. One day a big truck arrived with Dad's desk, some chairs, the impressive bookcase for those tin soldiers, and Mom's desk with the marble top. All of these pieces ended up in the living room and looked as if they always had been there—even in a modern house!

In any case, the next two years were uneventful and we all settled in to the many facets of small town living. Our neighbor Mr. King had a garage in which he kept large drums of vanilla. During the summers Marie-Anne and I worked for him, pouring the vanilla into small bottles for resale. He paid us 25 cents an hour. Dad had gotten us this gig thinking it was a great way for us to learn the meaning of a buck, early in life. We also did occasional babysitting for neighbors.

Dad took us three kids to mass every Sunday at Mt. Carmel church while Mom stayed home since she had never been religious. None of us wanted to go and Steve was too young to understand what it was all about, but Dad had promised his mother he would take us to mass. One day the priest ended his sermon by saying he had noticed some parishioners were leaving right after communion, before the world peace pledge. He then said that must mean those who left early must be communists. Dad, who had been among those who left early—not to avoid the pledge but to get out of the parking lot before all the other cars—got up from the bench and directed us three kids to follow him. That was the last time we ever went to mass. No one, not even a priest, was going to call Gabe Raphel a communist.

Dad's position at Polak's now required him to travel back to company headquarters in Amsterdam. Although it would have been easy for him to take a side trip to France a few times, he never did. Perhaps he still didn't feel comfortable going back "home." Each time he traveled abroad, he came home with stories about how backwards Europe was when compared to America.

Soon after we arrived in Middletown Mom met Michelle—a woman who lived right down the street and became one of her best friends. She was born in France, had lived there many years and was fluent. Her background was rather unusual; she had been orphaned early, ended up as a dancer in Paris, had lived through the Nazi occupation and then migrated to the US soon after the war ended. She had a child out of wedlock who died during infancy and was never able to have children again. One of the draws to my mother, in addition to the French angle, was that Steve was a toddler. Michelle doted on him. She was also an accomplished quilter and photographer. Marie-Anne and I spent hours with her as she taught us how to operate her cameras and develop film in her dark room. Like our Mom, Michelle was very petite, looked very French and had a lot of energy. Every day of the week she walked five miles from her house to the YMCA to swim in the indoor pool. She was very fit.

Aside from Michelle, Mom gained another close friend when the Mc Dermotts built a house at the end of our street. Claire Mc Dermott and Mom had coffee nearly every morning at one another's house. When Claire came to our house, her large Shepherd Erie would come too. While the two women shared their life's experiences in the house, Erie sat outside by the laundry door, without a leash, patiently waiting for Claire. No one could have broken into our house while he stood guard.

Claire came in very handy the first day Steve started nursery school. After Dr. Millman experienced several of his meltdowns during office visits, he strongly recommended nursery school as an antidote to Steve's anxieties related to new situations. When Steve learned where he was going that morning, Mom was physically unable to get him into the car. It took Claire, Mom and a third neighbor to do so. Claire had to hold him down in the back seat during the ride to school. As expected, Steve took a while to get used to nursery school but once he finally accepted his fate he became a model student.

So everything was going along quite well on Mountain Avenue. No complaints.

But then, right around Christmas 1959, Mom started acting very strange. The bedroom Marie-Anne and I shared was directly across the hall from our parents' room so we could tell when their conversations were heated. Recently there were quite a few of those. Then Mom started wearing sunglasses during dinner. One night she not only wore sunglasses but she smoked cigarettes rather than eat her dinner! We three kids just ate our dinner in silence. Dad kept saying:

"Minette, tu est vraiement ridicule. Mange ton dinner," (Minette you are really ridiculous. Eat your dinner.)

She took another long drag from her cigarette, ashes perilously dangling, and said not in a nice way:

"Tu m'emmerde. Je ferais ce que je veux." (You're pissing me off. I will do as I please.")

Then things got even stranger. One night, after Marie-Anne and I were asleep, Dad opened our bedroom door and said:

"Avez-vous vu votre mère?" ("Have you seen your mother?).

So now, he too had lost his mind! How did he lose track of her in the house?

Now this was a very cold night in February, and where did he find her? She was on the patio, smoking a cigarette, shivering in her night gown! It took him a while to convince her to come in from the cold and we could tell she was very pissed at him. We just didn't know what he had done to make her go outside in the frigid weather, just to have a cigarette – which she could have smoked in the house!

Marie-Anne and I could not understand why Mom was behaving this way, but we determined first to stay out of her way and second to be as helpful as possible so she wouldn't get even weirder. One day, as I was leaving for school, Mom was putting clothes into the washer and I told her I would help her with the laundry when I got home. She looked at me sunglasses on, lit cigarette perched between two fingers with ashes about to fall, and she said:

"Va-te-faire foutre."

I had no idea what that meant but it didn't sound nice. Since I never forgot those words, I looked them up in a French dictionary many years later. It was: go fuck yourself!

We didn't have to wait much longer to find out what was wrong with Mom. Turned out she was pregnant again and this time it wasn't planned. That's why she was out that cold night smoking on the balcony, hoping to have a miscarriage. But as hard as she tried, even with other means, the pregnancy lasted and we were told there would be another sibling that summer. Two year old Steve didn't catch the significance of this, but Marie-Anne and I were ecstatic about having another baby in the house. If we all survived Mom's pregnancy, there would be two American babies in the Raphel household!

Carole Kim Raphel was born on August 22, 1960, just one week before Marie-Anne and I started our first year of high school. She was named, at our father's request, for Carole Lombard the actress, but since none of us particularly liked that name we all started calling her Kim from the start and that stuck.

She had a lot of jet black hair and started screaming as soon as she came home. She kept screaming her first two years, suffering from ear infections, teething problems and allergic reactions to milk or some foods. Very quickly Marie-Anne and I decided this was not what we had in mind, especially since we now had a lot of social activities. So we weren't excited about staying home to babysit a screaming infant. Mom had other plans—she expected us to help whenever we were home from school. Steve was given a break because of his age.

I recall one of Kim's particularly bad illnesses when Dr. Millman came to the house (yes they still made house calls in the sixties). When she saw him, she got hysterical because she thought he came to give her a shot plus he was rather scary-looking—with little hair, bulging eyes and drooping cheeks. Kim's reaction caused her fever to spike and she went into convulsions. Mom, never one to behave rationally in a crisis, lost all composure and started screaming that her child was dying.

While saying "Mother Raphel, calm yourself!"Dr. Millman gave Kim a shot and soon she stopped screaming. Her fever was gone the next day and life went back to normal, until the next illness.

Besides a new sibling, in 1960 we added another member to our family—Oliver, a copper-colored dachshund with an attitude. As I've already mentioned, Mom and Dad had bred dachshunds in France and had always favored that breed. When they learned a friend needed a new home for her three year old dachshund, they decided to adopt him although Mom was rather cool to the idea.

Oliver would remain in our family for more than ten years, quickly claiming the top spot in the household. Although Dad was the dog lover, Oliver quickly became Mom's dog since she was home with him all day. He was even more tied to her than Steve was. Any time she left the house, even if she just went down the street to see Claire or Michelle, he used his long nose to open her closet sliding doors. He would then take every one of her shoes and scatter them throughout the house.

When she came home, he faced her with utter defiance, as if to say:

"There, you should know better than to leave me alone!"

Oliver was so possessive of Mom that it was difficult for Dad to gain access to the marital bed. Each night, she took Oliver to bed with her and turned off the light so Dad could sneak into the bed. If she didn't turn off the light, Oliver would bark and growl when Dad tried to get in bed.

One day Oliver was on Mom's lap at the dinner table (yes, she allowed that). Dad started taunting the dog from the other end of the glass rectangular table.

"That's my bone," he said to him.

Oliver, who was fixated on a lamb chop on Mom's plate, growled and bared his teeth. Dad kept taunting him. The dog took the bait. He leapt out of Mom's arms, sailed across the dining table and landed on top of his nemesis; growling and barking viciously. Dad was doubled over with laughter. All of us kids laughed hysterically. Mom did not think it was funny one bit as Oliver managed to trash whatever was on the table and in his flight path.

In addition to Oliver, we also experimented with a fish tank inherited from a neighbor moving out of state. Since my parents had birds in France but Mom now considered them bad luck, exotic fish seemed like a good alternative and far less work.

The tank was placed in a large, custom-made bookcase a carpenter built for one of the living room walls. We spent a considerable amount of time buying plants for the tank and researching the best types of easy-care fish to buy. Once the tank was set up and had tenants, Dad took on the responsibility of feeding the fish. Every day when he came home from work at precisely 5:10 PM, he went through the laundry room, then the kitchen and into the living room. He opened the closet next to the tank, took out the container of fish flakes and completed the feeding task. As Mom often said:

"Il est trés maniac, comme son frère," ("He is obsessive compulsive, like his brother".)

Unfortunately for the fish, two year old Kim, finally blessed with better health, was now actively exploring her surroundings. She was especially fascinated by the fish tank, and tall enough to see its habitants up close. One day she noticed a knob on top of the tank and decided to turn it. This resulted in raising the tank's water temperature so much all the fish were cooked. When Dad came home that day, he fed the dead fish. Two weeks later, he was still feeding the fish-less tank. Mom gave the fish tank away.

CHAPTER 13

BITTERSWEET RETURN
TO FRANCE

CATHERINE

At the beginning of the sixties, the Raphels were in high spirits and well adjusted to life in Middletown. Mom was meeting new people in town, using her French accent and unique childhood stories to charm audiences. Steve was in nursery school several days a week and Kim was done with her string of illnesses. Marie-Anne and I had totally adjusted to our new country and were busy with school and activities. Dad continued to impress his colleagues at Polak's; his salary and Christmas bonus grew yet again.

At dinner one night in December 1961, he stopped eating his re-heated chicken and announced we would all be going to France the following summer.

"Alors, nous avons une surprise pour vous — nous allons tous en France l'été prochain."

This didn't mean anything to Kim who was learning to speak English and knew just a few French words. It also didn't impress Steve since he didn't know anything about France. But Marie-Anne and I were very excited about going "back home" and seeing our relatives again. Although they never said, I suspected Mom and Dad were finally ready to go home again.

There weren't many people in Middletown who travelled abroad in the early sixties so when we told our classmates about the trip, they were very impressed. Marie-Anne and I were counting the days until we could see the family again. Mom was anxious about making the long plane trip with a five and not quite two year old but she knew there would be plenty of people in France who would help her with the young kids.

The plan was to leave right after the end of school. Dad could only stay two weeks since that's all the vacation time he had but the rest of us would stay for two months. In spite of Dad's short stay in France, he insisted that he and Mom should spend a few days in Portofino and Lake Como. Mom was concerned this would not be well received by some of our relatives, but Dad kept saying they deserved to treat themselves to their favorite spots, in light of the hardships they had endured. He certainly had a point.

Gabe and Claudine on the patio at home on Mountain Avenue, 1961

The flight was REALLY tedious, with a LONG layover at the Paris airport. Steve, who hadn't slept much on the flight, ended up falling asleep on a set of stairs and blocking traffic. Soon airport personnel arrived and asked Mom and Dad to move him. Mom, sleep deprived and not in the best mood, told the guy to get lost. To avoid a scene Dad picked up Steve and put him in a chair without waking him up. We arrived in Nice exhausted but thrilled to be greeted by Mamie Charlotte and Charles and Zaza. There were lots of hugs and tears as we all realized how much we had missed each other.

We stayed at L'Oustalet in Golfe-Juan since Charles and Zaza were at the Pin Pignou above Vallauris and it was nice for those of us who had lived there to relive some wonderful memories. We even went to our old school and walked around the village. All of this brought back the good times we had living in this paradise setting; at least it did for Marie-Anne and me because that's all we remembered. Perhaps Mom and Dad felt differently.

Although the sea was right across the street, we could not swim there as there were lots of very large rocks we couldn't climb to get to the water. No matter, we only had a very short car ride to the beach across the street from Lerina where we used to swim. When we went there the next day, we were shocked to see our grandmother's former home was now replaced by a hideous ten story condominium apartment building. Marie-Anne and I didn't know Mamie Charlotte had sold the house and we were very upset it was gone. Mom was crying like a baby and Dad had to console her. The only way we knew Lerina had once been in that spot was because the immense Magnolia tree was still there on the right side of the new building.

Our grandmother Mamie Charlotte was now living in Nice but she came to see us in Golfe-Juan several times a week. We had many rowdy family dinners that made us realize how lucky we had been then to live close to loved ones. Once again, the maid Alfreda cooked excellent meals using local produce and those delicious fresh chickens. It was hard to accept the store-bought American chicken had anything to do with this tender, moist and flavorful meat. We had almost forgotten what a charmed life we had in Golfe-Juan and how good French food was. One night we all went to Tetou for Bouillabaisse; the owner and his family welcomed us with big hugs but a small discount on the bill.

The Paris family also came to see us on the coast—Aunt Poussy, still known as Tante Peste (Aunt Pest), Uncle Pierre and his wife Aglaé and our cousin Roselyne. They kept saying how much Marie-Anne and I had changed; how impressed they were with our English. They were equally impressed we had not lost our French and thanked Mom and Dad for making sure we spoke french at home. Everyone fussed over Steve and Kim and more than one member of the family noted how large our family had become. It wasn't typical for French families to have four children; two was more the norm. At least that was the case in our "milieu" (circle).

Before he had to go back home, Dad was anxious to visit their friends the Simons who had adopted his dog Anouk. He wondered if she would remember him. Mom kept telling him it had been too long; he shouldn't expect too much. When we went into the house Anouk barked, as Dachshunds always do when someone appears, so she didn't recognize us. Then we all sat down and the adults started catching up on the past six years. Anouk stood in the middle of the room only looking at Dad. She must have stared at him for about ten minutes, and then she started coming toward his chair. She looked right in his eyes, then jumped up in his lap and sniffed his clothing, his hands and then started licking his cheeks. He was overjoyed and I saw tears in his eyes; clearly she remembered him. She had been his special dog and one of the many things he regretted when he left France. Seeing her again, and having her recognize him, was probably the highlight of Dad's trip.

The village had not changed much during our absence, except there were now a lot more people on the beach than I remembered. The same folks still worked in the restaurants and the markets. They all remembered us and made us feel like celebrities, pumping us for information about what it was like to live in America. Mom and Dad made sure to tell them how great their lives were there; how everything was so much easier than in France—like buying food all in one place rather than wasting time going to different specialty shops. They really poured it on; making sure everyone knew they were happier in America.

As we talked to the locals, I noticed Dad always mentioned he was now the chief perfumer for an international company and that he travelled quite a bit. Mom told them our house in Middletown was the biggest one on our street. When the Paris family came to visit, she made a big deal about the clothes she had brought which didn't require ironing because they were all made from synthetic materials. That really impressed the women in the family who said they hated to iron, which surprised me because I knew they all had maids who did their ironing.

I definitely got the impression Mom and Dad wanted everyone in Golfe-Juan to know they were glad they had moved to America. Since I didn't know then why they had left to begin with, I could only assume there were some bad feelings. Yet, there was no ignoring that it really was a beautiful part of the world to have come from.

We did not go back to Juliette-Antoinette because the house had been sold. Although a friend knew the new owners and asked if we wanted to visit, Dad declined; it was still too soon for him. It would likely have been too emotional.

We also spent time with our grandmother Juliette, who was now 76 years old and living in an apartment in Cannes with our aunt Marcelle and our uncle Claude. They were thrilled to meet Steve and Kim but it was obvious my grandmother mostly loved seeing our Dad. It was nice to see them again but there was not much to talk about with them—they just didn't want to hear about our new life. At one point I heard my grandmother ask

Dad when we would move back to France. He didn't answer but he hugged her.

There is one more memory I have of that summer—and it involves a boat ride, a handsome young man and my first experience with a sexual encounter. My friend Kaki Junot, who knew a lot of rich people on the French Riviera, invited Marie-Anne and me to go for a boat ride with some of her friends in Ville Franche-Sur-Mer, just southwest of Monaco.

I really don't remember much about that boat ride, not where we went nor how long we were on the boat. But I do remember Julien; a tall, handsome young man who took a special interest in me as soon as we boarded the small yacht. I had just turned 15 that May and he must have been about 18. At first he was mostly interested in hearing about my life in America and I was proud he had noticed me.

When we all decided to go for a swim, I took off my sun dress and I saw a different look in his eyes. I may have been young but I had the body of a grown woman and I could see he appreciated that. After a nice refreshing swim, it was time to head back. During the ride home, Julien offered to show me the stateroom below and, naturally, I went with him. That's when I got my first real French kiss, and that's also when I allowed a boy to touch me in places where I should not have been touched. But no one saw us so I didn't protest—what was the harm? Plus, it sure felt good. Almost as important, I was very thrilled he wanted to be with me!

Julien was the first in a series of handsome, persuasive young men I would partner with who would become sources of bad choices and regrets. Somewhat following in my father's careless management footsteps, I placed too much emphasis on personal gratification without concern for consequences. Just as these bad choices were Dad's Waterloo, they became mine as well.

I would return to France less than three years later, but not for a vacation. I went there to undo the first of two big mistakes.

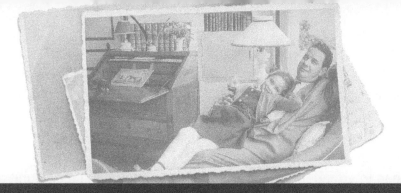

CHAPTER 14

CLAUDINE'S CANCER

CLAUDINE

I loved every minute of our summer in France. We were able to spend time with everyone in the family; even the ones who lived in Paris came down to Golfe-Juan to see us. There was so much to catch up on. They all wanted details of our life in America and were very pleased to see the girls had retained their French. Steve and Kim were a big hit and I had a lot of help with them. It was also terrific to taste delicious French meals again. I had forgotten how good French food is; how fresh the fruit and vegetables are and how a simple roasted chicken just melts in your mouth. For me, that trip was perfect; I no longer felt angry about what happened to make us leave. I was just thrilled to be with my family again, enjoying the summer in what had always been a pretty terrific place to live. The summer went by much too quickly but my mother and Zaza promised to come see us in America.

Soon after we got home, the girls started their sophomore year in high school. Steve was in kindergarten and Kim in nursery school two days a week. All of a sudden, I had more time to myself and this made me happy. Gabe's salary was increased again and we hired Mrs.Walker to clean the house each week. I was especially grateful for that.

At the same time, Gabe's international travel schedule increased because there were more perfumers' conferences he had to attend in Europe. Kim and Steve were still too young to be left behind with the girls so I could never accompany him on these trips, and that was a source of aggravation for me. Frankly, I considered these trips as vacations for Gabe while I had to stay home with the kids. I knew some of his colleagues from Polak's brought their wives along but they didn't have young kids like we did.

The next couple of years went by very quickly and everything was just as it should be for our family. No complaints, finally! I spent quite a bit of time with my neighbor Claire, so she had become my confidant. Any time I was afraid something bad would happen, which I thought about often, Claire would talk sense into me. I kept telling her that life was so good now; as good as it had been in France before everything was taken from us, that I feared something awful would happen again. Claire would laugh in that loud, throaty laugh of hers and she would say:

"Oh Claudine, don't be such a pessimist! You've got a terrific life and it's not going to change."

I wanted to believe her. We certainly had lived through our share of hard times but somehow I didn't think the good times would last; my fears were confirmed in 1964. One day, I felt a lump in my left breast while I was taking a bath. I was so terrified all I could do was cry and stay in that bath water until it was so cold I was shivering.

The next day I told Claire about the lump. Since she was always optimistic, she tried to assure me there was nothing to worry about but she urged me to go see Dr. Camillo, a local doctor who had a very good reputation. I decided not to tell Gabe until after I had seen the doctor.

Dr. Camillo examined me and asked a lot of questions about

my family's medical history and how many women had breast cancer. I could only recall one of my grandmothers. Then he told me there was a chance the lump could be benign and he would remove it. I would have a slight indentation in my breast where the lump had been. Since I would be under general anesthesia, the lump would be sent to the lab for an immediate examination. If it was malignant, he would remove the entire breast and the lymph nodes under my left arm. . I would not know the outcome of the surgery until I came out of anesthesia!

When Gabe got home that night and the kids were in bed, I told him about the lump and what I had learned from Dr. Camillo. Gabe's reaction was I didn't have cancer and most likely Dr. Camillo wanted to operate because he needed money to go on vacation! Since Gabe was never sick, he had almost no exposure to doctors and did not trust them. In fact, the only time he had relied on a doctor was when he dislocated his shoulder the day we left for America. Looking back on his reaction, I am certain that was just his way of dealing with hearing the news and being very afraid of my having cancer.

There were a few nervous weeks in our house while I was waiting for the surgery. Claire was the only one I could really talk to about my fears; what if I did not survive the illness even if I lost my breast? I had a two and a five year old. Who was going to raise them if I died? I did a lot of crying in her house and she tried to assure me it would all be fine in the end. But I kept thinking of our four kids, especially the two young ones. How would they manage without a mother?

A few weeks later, Gabe drove me to the hospital. When I woke up from the anesthesia, Dr. Camillo told me he had to remove my left breast and lymph nodes because the tumor was cancerous. I was shocked and became hysterical, so much so the nurse had to give me a sedative. When I was calm enough to talk, I asked Dr. Camillo a lot of questions about my recovery, whether I would need any further treatment and what my chances were for long term survival. Dr. Camillo was patient with me and kept saying that he was confident he had removed all of the cancer.

I asked Dr. Camillo to tell Gabe the outcome of the surgery; I was afraid how he would respond. When that conversation took place, Gabe's reaction was quite different from what I expected. He had a pained look on his face and started to cry. That's when I knew he had been just as scared as I was about this cancer.

Dr. Camillo said he had removed all of the cancer, but to be sure I would have to undergo radiation treatments. In 1962 only New York City hospitals used chemotherapy to treat cancer. There was no discussion about re-constructive surgery; that didn't happen back then. A very kind nurse told me where to buy a breast form to stuff into the left side of my bra. Every time someone new came into the room to talk about my life after this cancer surgery, all I wanted to do was crawl in a hole and push the clock back to that glorious summer in France.

I stayed in the hospital for two weeks and was grateful for the strong pain medication. When the girls came to see me, Catherine said I looked very pale. Marie-Anne said she thought I had gotten even smaller. They noticed there was a large glass container on the floor under my bed with red liquid in it. Catherine asked what it was and I told her it was the blood draining from the incision on my left side. When Marie-Anne heard that she nearly fainted. Gabe was also looking rather pale and worried. There was no more mention of Dr. Camillo's vacation money.

When I came home I stayed on the couch in the living room, surrounded by lots of flowers from neighbors and Gabe's co-workers. I was in a lot of pain and afraid to sleep in our bed in case Gabe got too close to my incision. Also, he needed his sleep to work; I could nap much of the day. Michelle took a picture of me on the couch and you can clearly see the sadness and fear in my eyes.

The girls were a lot of help when they got home from school and Claire and Michelle helped out during the day; driving Steve and Kim to school and making sure I ate and rested. I was afraid the cancer was not totally gone and that I would not survive. Only Michelle and Claire knew how terrified I was. I didn't want Gabe to know because then he too would worry.

When the radiation sessions started that was worse than anything that came before. After each treatment, I had excruciating pain; a burning like I had never felt before. I really tried to be brave but I would cry until the girls got home from school.

When the time came to remove the stitches, Gabe said he wanted one of the girls to come with us to Dr. Camillo's office. Since Marie-Anne nearly fainted at the sight of blood, Catherine was elected to come with us. I was glad she was there because when Dr. Camillo removed the bandages and my left side was exposed, I chose not to look down. However, I saw the look on Gabe's face; I knew I was maimed and from that point on he would look at me differently.

This happened in the spring of 1964. In late fall, my mother and stepfather Roger came to visit as they had promised the previous summer. They were the first of the French family to visit us in America, and it was wonderful to have them here. I had fully recuperated from the surgery and Gabe and I showed them around Middletown and introduced them to some of our new American friends. We even drove down to New York City and had dinner in a fancy restaurant, walked around Fifth Avenue and went to Times Square. My mother and stepfather were very impressed by the skyscrapers and all that the city had to offer. The language was a barrier since neither of them spoke English but my mother was very gracious to everyone and they all loved her. She was the best medicine for me.

Often during my convalescence I thought about the day in France when I went before a firing squad and that German soldier decided I was too young to die. Was that day my only chance of survival? Even though Dr. Camillo said he had removed all the cancer, could it come back in another form? And what about the cancer risk for my three daughters? Could this mean one of them might get this dreaded disease?

CHAPTER 15

WHY CAN'T I?

CATHERINE

Our family experienced a number of highs and lows during the sixties.

Among the highs were moving to Middletown, Kim's birth and our summer back in France; the biggest low was Mom's cancer. Although she had always been a serious drama queen and got hysterical over very little, Mom surprised us all during this crisis. She was very brave through the surgery and recuperation. The only time I saw evidence of her having cried was after the radiation treatments because they were so painful. What really helped her recovery was when Mamie Charlotte came to Middletown. Mom had always been Mamie's favorite and the two of them got along like sisters.

School was going well for all four of us kids. Steve was getting used to being in school all day and Kim adjusted quickly to nursery school. Marie-Anne and I had accumulated an impressive group of girl friends during our freshman year in high school. During our junior year the two of us, along with twelve of our girl friends, formed a group called the "Flirtatious Fourteens". We did it mainly to poke fun at a group of five boys in our school who started calling themselves "the Fab Five," in an attempt to match their popularity with the Beatles who were known as "the Fab Four".

When the Fab Four came to the US and were on the Ed Sullivan show on February 9, 1964 several of the Fab Fives came at our house to watch the show. Marie-Anne and I had a small TV in our bedroom and that's where we gathered since Dad always watched the show but didn't want to have a bunch of teenagers with him in the TV room. When the Beatles came on, we all started screaming and jumping up and down. The heaviest Fab Five executed a canon ball jump onto Marie-Anne's bed and broke it. For the rest of the year, the poor guy was teased about breaking that bed by simply landing on it; not for any other scandalous reason.

All but one of the Fab Fives was a football player and they were all pretty cocky. The "Fourteens" were a much more diverse group of young ladies—many of us were cheerleaders but others were also potential valedictorians, Junior Prom queens or designated "most likely to succeed". We were a formidable group and wore our "Fourteen" designations as badges of honor.

As far as Marie-Anne and I were concerned, high school should last forever. Every time our parents brought up going away to college, we kept insisting there was no reason for us to ever leave the area. We loved Middletown and there was a community college in town so we could enroll there. We weren't even interested in broadening our horizons by going to New York City to see a play or visit museums. All we wanted to do was spend time with our friends, continue our devotion to being cheerleaders and put off as long as possible this tedious thing called "growing up."

My grades were average at best, sometimes bordering on mediocre. Marie-Anne was a much better student so during her junior year Dad took her to Poughkeepsie, NY to interview at Vassar College. Someone at his work told him that was THE best women's college in the country so he figured that's where his daughter should go. During the interview the college admissions person asked Marie-Anne what she liked most about high school and in her still shy manner Marie-Anne said she especially loved cheerleading. Dad knew by the look on that admission person's face that Vassar was out of reach for his daughter.

Even though the Vassar trip was not successful, Dad insisted his daughters had to go to college for one important reason: so they would have something to fall back on in case their marriages didn't last. This was an interesting perspective coming from a self-described French chauvinist, but perhaps he had an ability to look into the future. He also dictated that we only consider women's colleges so that we could focus exclusively on our studies rather than on the opposite sex.

During the fall of my senior year, I started focusing on more than being a cheerleader and one of the Fourteens. I began cheering aggressively for a certain football player. We'll call him Dominic. He noticed me and I got the hoped-for response. Soon we were an item and I was wearing his Varsity Letter sweater. He wasn't one of the "Fab Fives" but he was super cool and had lots of friends. He was tall, had dark skin and black hair, piercing brown eyes, a chiseled face and a great body. When he looked at me, with his head slightly bent and a mischievous smile, I literally melted. Unlike many guys our age, he had his own car!

Dominic wasn't my first Middletown boyfriend. Back in my sophomore year, I had become involved with a nineteen year old who was repeating his senior year. He was the son of a doctor in town and lived in a large house on Highland Avenue so I thought my parents would approve. Instead they said he was much too old for me and obviously he was a loser since he hadn't graduated with his class. They told me to stop spending time with him. Since by then I was determined to ignore my parents' ridiculous rules, the loser and I spent time in his car in between my after school activities.

Loser or not, he did teach me some things that would have

shocked my parents and I naively chronicled these acts in my diary. Unfortunately, Mom found my diary and learned all about what happened in that car. Since I had already been told to stop seeing him, Mom was beside herself. She immediately curtailed my after-school activities and hovered over me like a helicopter. That ticked me off!

Honestly, I was boy crazy and not shy about expressing my admiration for the opposite sex. I also had developed a woman's body before my teens and had rather pronounced breasts. That got the boys' attention. Since my focus was on boys first, cheerleading second, and school last - my grades suffered.

Marie-Anne, on the other hand, did not develop a woman's body until she was in college. She also wasn't interested in boys until her senior year. She was still shy and only comfortable around other girls. Since she and I were very different in this respect it was difficult for me to convince our parents that girls our age cared a lot about the opposite sex.

When Dominic and I got together that fall, Mom and Dad came up with all sorts of reasons why I couldn't ride in his car. Unwilling to accept their position on this, I pressed the issue, often continuing to argue by repeating "Why can't I?"

Since riding in his car was out of the question, going on dates was impossible and we had few opportunities to be alone. It never occurred to me that my parents might have a legitimate reason for preventing us from being alone. All I knew was that I was completely infatuated with him and very unhappy when I couldn't be with him. When I wasn't suffocating him with kisses, I was telling him how great he was. Unlike some other sixties young women, I was not at all a feminist; I believed he defined me. Without him, I was nothing; I was totally subservient and considered Dominic far superior to me in capabilities and intellect. Basically, I was a doormat when it came to the opposite sex and would remain so for many years.

Eventually I wore my parents down and they finally agreed

I could go out with Dominic one night on the weekend. To celebrate, he surprised me with tickets to see Little Anthony and the Imperials, a very popular 60s group who were performing in Newburgh about 25 miles from Middletown. The show unfortunately did not start until 9 PM and my curfew was 11 PM. I begged Mom and Dad to extend the curfew just this time but they refused. Mom also pointed out that the weather could be unpredictable because it was winter. Sure enough on the day of the show, the forecast was calling for snow that evening.

We went anyway, in spite of Mom's arguments against it, and the group did not disappoint. They were spectacular and we wished we could have stayed for the second set but knew that was beyond my curfew. Although there was no hint of snow during our drive to Newburgh, when we left the theater it was obvious it had been snowing most of the time we were in the building. Since we had to be home quickly, Dominic drove too fast and we skidded into a ditch. We waited quite a while for another car and managed to get help pushing out of that snow drift. In the end, I got home a little after midnight and Mom was waiting for me in the laundry room. As Dominic was kissing me goodnight, the door burst open and she grabbed me by the collar and said:

"Say goodbye to her Dominic. You won't be seeing her for a while!"

The next morning I learned my punishment; I was grounded for six months! I tried to explain how we ended up being late but Mom kept saying she had warned me about the weather and that I should not have gone. That's when I first heard the words "unintended consequences."

Being grounded for six months meant I would miss senior year parties and the senior prom. I was devastated and spent a lot of time in my room crying about how unfair this was. Mom would not budge but after a couple of months of good behavior, the punishment was lifted. Dad had intervened on my behalf.

This was not the first time he had gone to bat for me. During Junior Year, Marie-Anne and I were both running for Junior Prom attendant. From a large group of contestants, twelve of us would be chosen for the Junior Prom King and Queen Court. I was voted one of those twelve attendants. Marie-Anne was not and when she came home crying about it, Mom said I should decline this honor. When Dad came home from work that night and learned what had taken place, he said it was not right to ask me to decline and I was allowed to be an attendant.

Aside from these personal stories, the most memorable event that happened during our senior year was the day President Kennedy was shot. Like most people of our generation, I remember exactly where I was when the principal announced over the PA system that he had died. I was in study hall and we were all immediately sent home. I was at my locker getting my coat when my friend Sandy ran toward me with a stricken look on her face, screaming:

"Do you know what this means?"

I couldn't answer since all I knew what that our president was dead. But she said:

"It means Johnson will now be our president!"

As much as I was shocked and saddened over Kennedy's death—we were very big Kennedy fans in our house—that simply didn't register for me. So I said "So?"

She proceeded to tell me how different Johnson was from Kennedy and how things were going to change in our country because of this. I was incredibly impressed that one of my friends knew so much about politics she could provide this context. I hadn't even been aware that Johnson was next in line. That should tell you how much I retained in Mrs. Reardon's Social Studies class.

The following week was a blur, as most of us were glued to the television (black and white of course). We cried when we saw Jackie and the kids, especially when John John saluted his father's coffin, and we gasped when Jack Ruby shot Lee Harvey Oswald, in real time!

I managed to get through the rest of senior year without breaking curfew and otherwise stayed out of trouble. Rather than spending the night at a girl friend's house after the senior prom, which is what my parents thought I was doing, Dominic and I went to a motel. I had just turned 17, so if my parents learned we had spent the night together they would have known sex was included. They could have had Dominic arrested since I was a minor. Only a handful of my friends knew we had spent the night together; I hadn't even told Marie-Anne.

In the fall, Marie-Anne was to begin her freshman year at Skidmore College in Saratoga Springs, New York. The week before her departure, she took to her bed. She would not eat and she would not tell us what was wrong. She just kept crying. Even though she had been excited about going away to college, the reality hit her hard. She was still very shy and had difficulties making new friends and adjusting to change.

Mom spent a lot of time talking to her; eventually getting her to eat some food and trying to convince her that the college years were going to be the best ones of her life. Finally the day she dreaded was here and Mom and Dad drove her to school. We feared she would refuse to stay there but she surprised us all. Not only was her mood different when she got on campus, but she seemed fine when our parents left. When we spoke to her the next day, she said she was settled in and already had made some friends. We all breathed a large sigh of relief.

I was not at all jealous that Marie-Anne went away to college and I had to stay home. I had only applied to one college in Boston and was not accepted so I started classes at the local community college. The best part of staying in town was that I could still spend time with Dominic because he had not yet decided what he was going to do with his life. Since I was only 17 when I graduated from high school, and had demonstrated a tendency to do stupid things, my parents were glad I stayed home so they could keep an eye on me.

In retrospect, had my parents and I been able to look into the future we would have learned that my staying home would lead to a series of events that haunted me for years and would become the source of my greatest regret.

CHAPTER 16

BETWEEN A ROCK AND A HARD PLACE

CATHERINE

At the beginning of 1965, all of us kids were doing well and there was little drama in the house. Marie-Anne was having a great year at college and had made lots of friends. When her college had dances with boys from surrounding colleges, she started dating. Steve came home from Catholic school one day and asked Mom for more money for the missions or he'd be assigned more homework. The very next day, he was yanked out of that school. This, in addition to our boycotting church because we were accused of being communists, led to our final divorce from the Catholic Church.

As for me, life was very good. I was enjoying having a bedroom to myself and pleased that college studies were no more demanding than high school. Other than devoting part of the week to a job at Green's Department Store in town, I spent the rest of my free time with Dominic. Since neither of us had money for a motel room, we had only repeated our senior prom activity a couple of times in the back seat of his car. Because this just happened a few times we hadn't bothered with birth control.

One day in late February of 1965, I woke up feeling nauseous. Initially, I chalked it up to a stomach virus but it persisted for days. I should also mention that my period hadn't come when it should have.

After a couple of weeks of agony, I told Dominic I thought we had a problem. We talked about the "what if" in case I was pregnant but other than that we didn't put a plan in place. We were both in denial. Finally, when I had missed my second period I told him I should see a doctor to find out for sure. There were no instant pregnancy tests in those days.

We were just about to make an appointment with a doctor out of town when Mom cornered me in the kitchen as soon as I came home from school one day.

"I've been checking the little garbage in your bathroom," she tells me, hands on hips and looking accusatory, "and I haven't seen any soiled napkins in a while."

I've always been a bad liar and this time was no exception. Instead of coming up with a good excuse, I started stuttering and couldn't form an adequate response.

"Tell me right now! Do you have any reason to think you might be pregnant?"

That's when I burst into tears and nodded.

It was a set up. Dad had been hovering outside so Mom could corner me. She went to get him. I was frozen in place in the kitchen as he walked in at a great rate of speed, almost yelling:

"Let's get her to a doctor and, depending on what we learn, we'll send her to France."

At first I didn't know why they were sending me to France, so I asked.

"Because you're not going to have this baby," Mom said. "You will have an abortion!"

I was stunned. I hadn't thought of that at all. During our conversations, Dominic and I talked about getting married and having the baby or giving the baby up for adoption. At no time had we discussed abortion. Our family had left the Catholic Church but he was a devout follower.

The next several days were a blur and I don't think I slept at all. Mom took me to the doctor and I had my first internal exam (not fun) and a pregnancy test, which came back positive. I was in the early stages of pregnancy.

I was allowed to call Dominic to tell him I was indeed pregnant and I would be going to France for an abortion. I was only allowed to talk to him for a minute. All he had a chance to say was that he wanted to talk to my parents but they refused to get on the phone. They made me hang up on him and told me he was permanently out of my life.

Since I would not be 18 until May, I initially was not given any choice about my pregnancy. Mom wrote to Mamie Charlotte and asked if my step grandfather, who was an orthodontist in Nice, knew someone who could "take care of my condition."

In addition to having no choices, I had to tell my professors I would be missing a few weeks of classes and I was kept in the house. I couldn't see any of my friends. When Mom was out, I managed to call Dominic and he told me he had gone to Dad's office to talk to him but he had been sent away.

Within two weeks Mamie Charlotte wrote back to Mom that they had found a doctor and I could come to France right away. She advised Mom to make travel arrangements immediately as the price of the procedure would increase the longer we waited.

I was terrified about what was happening and felt totally alone. I was ashamed that I had been so naïve (who believes you'll get pregnant until it happens?). Since we'd had sex so few times, I never thought I would get pregnant so easily. Marie-Anne was the only other person I talked to once Mom and Dad knew. During that phone conversation, all I could do was cry. I couldn't explain how scared or how conflicted I was over not having any choices. Since she didn't know we had stayed in a motel the night of the prom, she was shocked to learn we had been having sex

AND that I was pregnant. She seemed very distant during that phone call, but she really couldn't relate to my situation.

I didn't want any of our friends to know since no one in our group had gotten pregnant. If any of the others were having sex, no one admitted it and maybe they were using birth control. Or maybe I was just unlucky. Certainly no one I knew had gone to another country for an abortion!

A few nights before I was scheduled to leave for France Mom came into my room and told me what to expect during the abortion. She succeeded in scaring me even more. After this "heart to heart talk," Mom and Dad must have had conversations about this because the next night Dad came into my room and said:

"Even though legally you have no choice in this matter your mother and I have decided that we should not force you to have an abortion. You can either choose to have the baby and give it up for adoption or you can marry Dominic, if he'll have you. But if you choose to marry him you can say goodbye to your family. You will never see any of us again."

I didn't need a lot of time to decide. I didn't want to spend the rest of my life ex-communicated from my family. The following week Dad drove me to Kennedy Airport. I was very happy Mom didn't come along because I had some rare alone time with Dad.

"You've made the right decision. I know you will look back on this someday and admit you were too young to have a child," he said.

I could only nod my head and cry some more. I felt empty, scared and wished this was all just a nightmare.

"Everyone makes mistakes, and that's how you learn" Dad said. "I made mistakes when I was young, and I learned from them because they cost me a lot."

That's when he told me how he had trusted the wrong people, how that led to the bankruptcy and how painful it was to leave France and start all over again in America.

"I was young, naïve and arrogant. I really believed nothing bad would ever come my way because I was so smart," he confessed. "We had a fabulous life in France and because of my lack of judgment, I threw it all away. The whole family paid for that."

I was speechless when he stopped talking. All this time I never knew why they left France. Once Marie-Anne and I came to the states, it didn't matter why our lives had changed so much. We were back with our parents and that's all that mattered.

I resolved to remember Dad's words of wisdom and to make sure I never screwed up again.

Dad gave me a very long hug before I boarded the flight and he told me how much he loved me. He said Mom loved me just as much and all she wanted was the best for me.

Mamie Charlotte and Roger met me at the airport in Nice and surrounded me with love. Mamie told me that she had several abortions herself because my real grandfather, the other Roger, would appear after an absence and convince her she was his only love. Then he would disappear and soon after she would be pregnant and the last thing she needed was another child. She re-assured me the procedure was painless and would be over quickly. I wanted to tell her that Mom had told me something quite different but for once I decided to keep quiet.

I spent the first couple of days in Nice at Mamie Charlotte's house getting over the jet lag. Then my step grandfather took me to see the doctor who would perform the abortion. That was the most embarrassing part because my step grandfather insisted on staying with me in the examining room when I got my second internal exam. That was just too weird because Roger was an orthodontist! But in time I understood that he was protecting me—making sure the doctor behaved.

Abortion was illegal in France in 1965 so I don't know how

my step grandfather found a willing doctor. The day before the surgery, the doctor inserted a device to dilate my cervix but that is the only time I felt pain and it didn't last long. The abortion was done under anesthesia so I felt nothing. I had a very safe kind of procedure; certainly not the kind Mom had described.

After a few days of rest, Mamie Charlotte arranged a get together with my friend Kaki Junot and her mother Lidy. Since I had seen her last, Kaki had become engaged and soon would marry. I was thrilled for her and told her so. No one ever mentioned the reason for my trip and I was grateful for that. I assumed they knew; why else would I have come alone at this time of year? Kaky gave me a necklace as a souvenir of my trip; a gesture often practiced in France when guests came to visit. It is oval shaped and solid on the exterior facing side but when you turn it over there is a profile of the Virgin Mary and a child. I have treasured that necklace ever since that day and I wear it regularly.

After a few more days of Mamie Charlotte's pampering I flew home, Dad was waiting for me at the airport and I was glad Mom hadn't come with him. Again, he re-assured me I had made the right decision and that someday I would appreciate the fact that they had "encouraged" me to choose this option.

All I wanted to do was erase the whole sordid affair from my mind. What I didn't know, was how I was going to handle being back in Middletown, back to my former life without Dominic. I was still very much in love with him and I couldn't help thinking about what our life would have been like had we become a family.

I didn't have to wait long to figure out how to handle life without Dominic. My first month home, I learned from one of his friends that he had decided to join the marines. He was leaving soon for boot camp and wanted to see me before he left. Through this friend, we arranged to meet in the auditorium at the college I was attending, knowing there would be no one there during the day. I was very nervous about doing this, afraid we would be caught or afraid he would be very angry with me for having gone to France for the abortion.

When I got to the auditorium, I saw him and ran into his arms. There was a lot of crying and kissing and I knew we still loved each other very much. When I told him I had to choose between going to France and never seeing my family again, he understood and told me he was not angry. We stayed in the auditorium for about an hour, while he told me all about his decision to become a marine.

For the next several weeks before Dominic left for boot camp, we arranged through friends to spend time together. When he left, we promised to find a way to stay in touch. I had decided that I would focus on my studies to earn grades good enough to transfer to a college out of town next year and away from my parents' scrutiny.

The rest of the year brought change for both Dominic and me. I was accepted at Russell Sage, a women's college in Troy, New York but Dominic didn't fare that well. He didn't make it through boot camp and was sent home. I wondered how much the abortion had weighed on him, making it difficult for him to complete the difficult marine training.

He called me at college that fall and said he'd signed up for the Coast Guard since he didn't know what else to do. That meant he could be stationed anywhere in the country and it would be difficult for us to see each other on a regular basis.

My new college was a step up from my former one because I was boarding there, away from my parents' rules. The campus, however, wasn't very appealing. Although founded in 1916, not much had been added to the infrastructure by 1965. Since the brick, multi-story rectangular-shaped dorms were placed close together near the highway, you could hear speeding cars and trucks almost all the time. The rest of the campus, though further away from the highway, didn't have many trees or green spaces since it was in the city. Since that time, the college has significantly improved its facilities and is quite different from the way it was during my tenure.

My sophomore year was long on boredom and short on pleasure. One of the few highlights was my roommate Pam who was a very kind person and determined to make me laugh. I confided in her about Dominic and the abortion and she was shocked and sorry for me. Halfway through the year Toby, who lived on our floor, moved in with us because she couldn't stand her roommate. She packed her clothes and dragged her mattress to our room and that was that. Every night felt like a pajama party but somehow we managed to maintain good grades. The hall monitor was very accommodating and didn't turn us in although we were breaking the rule of only two girls in one room.

Aside from close friendships, another good memory from Russell Sage is the delicious cafeteria food. The chef was a local guy who worked on Cape Cod during the summer months and moved back to the Troy area each fall when the restaurant closed. Although working with a limited budget, he served up food that was equal to fine dining. Compared to the food cooked at home, I considered it worthy of five stars.

That fall of 1965 we were in the blackout that left about 30 million people without power for up to 12 hours on the East Coast. Chef even managed to feed us well that night, as we ate by candle light.

As far as dates that year, I counted them on one hand. Although there were many opportunities to meet boys from the other college in Troy—Rensselear Polytechnic Institute, known as RPI—I was rarely interested. Many of my classmates tried to fix me up, but I usually declined. I was still very much in love with Dominic and didn't want to invest in anyone else.

In the spring of 1966 Dad decided I should transfer to Marie-Anne's college, without asking for my opinion. Although the two schools were less than one hour apart, he said having us together would facilitate delivering us to school and bringing us home for vacations. Dad was very practical when it came to reducing the time spent on activities that didn't interest him.

Since I had earned good grades at Sage and my sister was a student at Skidmore, I was accepted for the fall term. I was sorry to leave Pam and Toby but excited about being at Marie-Anne's school. I had spent several weekends there during the year and already knew some of her friends; plus the campus was beautiful.

I came home before the end of May and lined up a job at Kassel Brothers, the other clothing store in Middletown. Dominic had a short leave and came home soon after me. We managed to steal a few hours together before he went back to where he was stationed. Since I hadn't dated much that year, and certainly hadn't slept with anyone else, birth control was not on my radar. One of the few times we got together we had sex, again unprotected. What could go wrong that one time?

The next month my period never came.

CHAPTER 17

STOP! IN THE NAME OF LOVE

CATHERINE

There is no legitimate excuse for my extremely poor lack of judgment in 1966. After the stress of the first pregnancy and abortion I should have taken precautions every time I had sex, regardless of how rarely it happened. Obviously, I was very fertile so birth control was mandatory for me. I was beyond foolish and I believe my obsession with Dominic played a big role. I simply ignored the potential for unintended consequences.

I have blocked out many details from that summer of 1966, with good reason. I do recall, however, the first decision I made was this time no one would know I was pregnant. Somehow, I would have to figure this out by myself. I had messed up once, and Mom and Dad had financially and emotionally paid for that mistake. I was not going to put them through that a second time, and I was not going to walk away from the college degree I now really wanted. That meant I had to have another abortion to keep the pregnancy a secret.

I saw a doctor in the town next to Middletown and he confirmed I was pregnant. Like Mom did back in 1959, I spent the next month trying to engage in activities that might result in a miscarriage. When the department store where I worked received heavy containers of winter clothing, I volunteered to take the items to the storage area hoping the strain would have an impact. I also drank Castor oil until I threw up. Then I read in a magazine that a woman had a miscarriage when she jumped out of a tree. So I climbed a tree and jumped, many times. Nothing worked.

By the end of July, I was desperate and knew I had to find someone who had a connection for me. I confided in a high school friend who knew someone who lived in Manhattan. I thought she might know of a doctor who performed abortions.

I wrote to Dominic and told him that once again I was pregnant. He didn't write back for quite a while and when he did I could tell from his reply that he was angry. He didn't provide any comfort or financial assistance so I knew I was really on my own.

The Manhattan contact confirmed she had a connection and admitted she had used this doctor's services so she could vouch for him. Then she told me I could stay in her apartment if I decided to have this done. I accepted her offer and we decided on a time frame that was best for her schedule. I called the doctor and made the appointment.

Now I had to figure out how to get out of Middletown for a couple of days, using an excuse that made sense to my parents. To do this, I had to rely on another friend whose parents had a cabin on a lake. She was willing to vouch she invited me to spend the weekend with them. This is the only part that was painless; everything fell into place quickly and no one suspected it was all a lie. I even managed to hide my morning sickness from Mom.

My lake cabin friend picked me up at home and took me to the bus station in town. Less than two hours later I was in the Manhattan apartment; the procedure was scheduled for the next day.

The rest of the weekend is almost impossible to put into words, except for the parts that I can't erase.

I remember riding the subway to the Bronx. I was so scared

of what I was about to face that I forgot about the nausea that had been my companion for weeks. Once I reached my destination, I almost couldn't go through with it. The building was a very run down brownstone with wooden steps that cried out for repair. On the porch, I noticed a collection of discarded pots with the remains of forgotten dead plants. The door bell did not work so I had to pound on the door. A middle-aged black man opened the door and confirmed he was the doctor. There was no small talk. He handed me a gown and told me to take everything off. Then he strapped me down on a table that had a rubber pad on it. I remember there was no one else there; no nurse, no receptionist. He told me he would insert a plastic tube inside my cervix, all the while stroking my pubic area. He then began the painful procedure which I have mostly blotted out. But I will always remember that while he was inserting the tube, the Supremes were singing loudly in the next room:

"Stop! In the Name of Love; before you break my heart— think it o over"

The procedure took less than ten minutes. I gave him $200 and he told me to get home quickly because I would start to bleed soon. I was too scared to admit I had an hour ride on the subway.

I started to bleed halfway through the train ride. Luckily I had a seat or I might have fainted. By the time I reached the apartment blood was dripping down my legs. My guardian angel put me to bed and gave me some aspirin for the cramps, which she said would get stronger soon. I was very glad she had been through this before since the doctor hadn't given me any medical advice.

I will not provide any more details except to say that the pains did get stronger and I miscarried hours later. But I paid a severe penalty; I have retained a visual that my consciousness can never erase. To my guardian angel: I am forever indebted to you for taking me in and keeping me from losing my sanity that night. I could not have done this without your kindness and your care. When I dare think back to that day, I realize I was very lucky; I didn't bleed to death on the subway.

I was so traumatized by this I didn't think about Dominic at all during those two days. When I got back home, I was just grateful to be alive and that no one knew where I had been. I resolved to get over my Dominic obsession and to never let this happen again. I also decided to stay clear of boys for a long, long time. That way, I would stay out of danger.

CHAPTER 18

HOT TOWN SUMMER IN THE CITY

CATHERINE

The dreadful summer of '66 ended and Marie-Anne and I started our junior year at Skidmore College in the fall. The country was erupting because of the sixties youth movement with frequent demonstrations against the Vietnam War as well as marches in support of Civil Rights. Skidmore was a small liberal arts women's college in Saratoga Springs, New York so we didn't have the kind of sit-ins that occurred at the nation's universities.

The college had launched a successful capital funds campaign at the beginning of the sixties and was in the process of building a brand new campus on the outskirts of town, which would open the following year. Marie-Anne and I would be the first class to live on the new campus our senior year. We were in separate dorms on the "old" campus for our junior year but spent a lot of time together outside of classes. She majored in Bio Chemistry while I chose Business Administration, with an emphasis on Advertising. I already knew a lot of Marie-Anne's friends there, so transferring to Skidmore was pretty easy.

Since I was starting as a junior, I couldn't choose my dorm

or roommate and I was put into a small single room in the French house. I suspected the rationale was that I could help the other residents with their French accents. As it turned out many weirdoes were assigned to that dorm, and none of them wanted to speak French. So what was the point of my being there?

Within a month, I was pleading my case to the housing administrator and succeeded in getting out of that dorm. Luckily a spot became available in Skidmore Hall, one of the college's oldest and biggest dorms; a beautiful piece of architecture. I escaped from a tiny room in the French house to sharing a large room whose former occupant had been unable to cope with college. I later realized it might have been due to the unique freshman who was now my roommate.

A true free spirit Kelsey spent her entire freshman year playing the guitar and regaling me with stories about growing up in a rich family in Greenwich, Connecticut. She was extremely bright, had a great sense of humor and could spin a wonderful story. She was exactly what I needed to get over Dominic. Since I was determined to get that college degree, however, I often escaped to the library to study. As you might expect, Kelsey was not asked back for her sophomore year but I have every expectation that she succeeded in life, somehow.

My classes were not difficult and I resolved to get good grades and stay out of trouble. I was also determined to get Dominic out of my system. I had a fair number of dates, in spite of being at a girls'college, but nothing that turned into a relationship.

When I went home for Easter break, I ran into my high school friend Sally, who had been one of the Flirtatious Fourteens. She was staying at Barnard for summer school and needed a roommate. I hadn't made plans for the summer yet so when she asked if I was interested I said I would need my parents' approval. It's not that I didn't want to live in Middletown that summer; I just didn't want to run into Dominic.

Mom and Dad surprised me. They said I could live in the city if I found a good job that covered my living expenses and left me enough spending money for the school year.

"I think having a job in the city will look very good on your resume when you graduate," Dad said. That's when he told me how important a resume had been for him to find work in America.

During the spring term I had enrolled in a market research class as part of my advertising focus. That decision would serve me well. TIME Inc. came to our campus that spring to interview candidates for summer internships. Lucky for me there was an opening in their market research department. Since I had taken the course, I applied for the internship and got it. I was thrilled and considered this a clear sign that things were looking up for me. No more bad luck.

Sally had found an apartment at the corner of 110th and Riverside Drive, very near the Columbia and Barnard campuses. I was looking forward to a new experience, but I was apprehensive about living in the city. But since Sally had been at Barnard for a couple of years, she could be my guide.

Mom drove me down to the city and spent the ride reminding me of the obvious:

"The city is a dangerous place; make sure you are not out alone at night."

"Take public transportation; do not rely on taxis."

"Keep to a budget so you don't spend your entire salary."

She also took the opportunity to remind me of the past:

"At least we don't have to worry about you getting pregnant since you're on the pill now," she added pointedly. (Our family doctor had prescribed the pill to regulate my period; it certainly was not because I was sleeping around.)

When we got to 380 Riverside Drive, Mom parked the car and we went into the large foyer looking for the doorman. We told him we were moving into 8F and gave him Sally's name so he could call her on the intercom.

We rode the elevator to the eighth floor and knocked on 8F. Sally opened the door and greeted us with her twinkling baby blue eyes and big smile.

"I'm so glad you're here. Welcome to Manhattan and the upper West Side. Let me give you the ten cent tour," she said.

There was a small bedroom almost immediately to the right of the front door, which Sally suggested should be my room since I had to keep regular hours. She then led us down the hall to a good-sized living room. It had dramatic large windows looking out on Riverside Drive and the Hudson River beyond it. To its left was another bedroom and behind it the eat-in kitchen. The apartment was minimally furnished, in need of painting and new carpeting and had a strange sweet odor. It was perfect!

"We really got lucky," Sally explained."Two of my Barnard friends who lease this apartment are abroad for the summer and they needed to sublet it until they get home. It's a great location."

Mom, Sally and I brought my stuff in from the car and I put my clothes in the closet of the small bedroom. Mom gave me a long hug before she left.

"Remember to call us at least once a week, and PLEASE be sure to save money for school," she said as she walked out the door.

That night, my new life began. I met some of Sally's friends, including Brian, a tall, burly-looking guy with red curly hair and a charming smile. He looked me over and asked:

"Hey doll, want to be my summer-time girlfriend?"

He seemed harmless and before I knew it, I was telling him a lot more about myself than I should admit to a stranger.

We learned we both loved James Brown and he invited me to go with him the following weekend to see him at the Apollo Theater in Harlem. I knew very little about Harlem but I had heard it was not a very safe place. This was confirmed when Brian announced his friend Jim would accompany us so there would be two of them to "protect me." That comment was made jokingly, but still…

I stayed up much later than I wanted to that first night, but it was worth it as I began to relax in my new environment. I also started thinking this could be the best summer of my life, and would help me get over Dominic.

The next morning was my first day of work at TIME Inc. I rode the IRT Broadway local down to Sixth Avenue and 50th street and stepped into the skyscraper, looking very much like a nervous college kid trying to make an impression. I still remember what I wore that day: a light gray, A-line linen dress with a large white collar and yellow piping and patent leather shoes that matched my purse.

I rode up the elevator with people who were much older than I was and looked far more self-assured. Soon Mandy Sullivan, my supervisor, introduced herself. She had been at TIME for four years, starting as a secretary and had moved up to assistant market analyst. I would be analyzing college readership surveys, she told me, and also assist her with other projects. I had a small office across from hers. At lunch she invited me to join her and even picked up the tab, using her expense account. I thought I had died and gone to heaven. Here I was in Manhattan, the greatest city in the world, working at a major news magazine! I was beside myself with joy. Finally, I was getting lucky!

My first week went by quickly and everything that seemed new and different were beginning to feel almost familiar—from the walk down the street to the subway, then the ride to TIME and the elevator to my little office. When I spoke to Mom and Dad at the end of the week, I told them it had been a terrific week, that my job was exciting, my supervisor super nice and the apartment was perfect.

As expected Mom reminded me to save my money, and I told her first I had to get paid!

I made sure NOT to tell them I was going to Harlem for a concert that night.

When Brian came for me, I had shed my work clothes and had on skin-tight black bell bottom pants with a light gray stripe, a loose fitting blouse and Jesus sandals (the cool footwear of the 60s). My hair was halfway down to my waste, but not tied in a pony tail as I wore it for work. I wanted to look like a hippie—my favorite kind of person—and I succeeded when Brian said:

"You look like you belong in a rock band. Are you trying to be like Janis Joplin?"

We met Brian's friend Jim at the subway stop and rode up to 125th. From the short subway walk, we could see a long line waiting to get into the Apollo. We got in line and were the only white people there. I was happy two big guys were with me but realized very quickly I would not need protection. Everyone there was in a good mood, just looking forward to a great concert. Shortly after we got in line a woman came up to us and asked if we wanted to buy her tickets because she had bought too many. We gladly accepted to buy them and got into the other shorter line for ticket holders. Soon we were in our seats.

The next three hours delivered the best concert I would ever attend. The Godfather of Soul gave us uninterrupted screeching, pleading, crying and gyrating—with the audience singing, dancing and staying on our feet the whole time. It was magical and I never felt out of place—even though the three of us remained the only whites in the theater. That memory has stayed with me for years, confirming that racial differences don't matter when you share a common interest or passion.

The following weekend Brian had another first for me. He brought a copy of the Beatles' new album—Sergeant Pepper's Lonely Hearts Club band—and insisted the only way to hear the cut "A Day in the Life" ("I read the news today, oh boy...") was to be stoned so the song could last even longer. I had never smoked pot before but I didn't tell him. I have to say he was right; that song lasted forever as did my first high. For years afterward every time I heard that song, I would think of Brian and how lucky I was to have met him that summer.

Coast to coast the hippie revolution was in full swing and young people were in charge. It was the summer of love in San Francisco—hippies were taking over the Haight Ashbury neighborhood and Scott Mc Kenzie's "San Francisco" was telling us "If you're going to San Francisco, be sure to wear some flowers in your hair". The Lovin' Spoonful's "Hot town, summer in the City" was a big hit and hippies swarmed the East and West Villages as if looking for hives. It was a world I had not yet joined, but I was eager to do so. I wanted to be Janis Joplin to sing and dance the way she did. I was becoming another person, someone who was forgetting about Dominic.

For much of June, I was the consummate Skidmore professional and TIME intern during the day, but at night I became Janis. With Brian and some of his friends, I spent nights in the West village mingling with street kids, taking recreational drugs and dancing to rock and roll. Before the end of the summer, strangers came into my life that nearly took me over to that side for good.

CHAPTER 19

THE DANGER ZONE

CATHERINE

Sally spent a weekend in Middletown in July and came back with an interesting story. Through one of our high school friends she met two guys who were visiting from Boston, on their way to San Francisco. Jason and Allen were street kids she said, with no discernable connections or aspirations.

"You would love Jason. He is 100% American Indian, Cherokee I think, and is absolutely gorgeous" Sally told me. "I hope you don't mind, I've given them our address. They might stop by on their way out to the West Coast".

Although Sally seemed excited about these guys showing up, I forgot about them. I spent the next two weeks still thoroughly enjoying my new life—posing as a professional during the day at TIME and becoming a hippy at night with Brian and others either in the Village or at our neighborhood hangouts. At the top of that list was the Gold Rail, a Morningside Heights bar on the corner of Broadway and 112th street that had the best cheeseburgers for little money. Our other local food monger was Mama Joy's, a small bodega that made outrageously good sandwiches.

The summer was delivering in spades; I was earning a decent salary and YES MOM I was saving enough of it. I was enjoying my research job and I managed to impress some of the account executives on my floor; enough to secure lunch invitations several times a week (expense account funded). If I failed to be invited, there was always the Horn and Hardart automat across the street from the Time and Life Building, where I bought a Dannon yoghurt for 19 cents and a piece of lemon meringue pie for 45 cents, and that was enough lunch for me.

Brian had become my best buddy; he didn't expect anything more than friendship. He was still reeling from a recent break up and I was trying to forget Dominic. So the relationship was working for both of us and he was showing me the best parts of Manhattan.

The only negative to the city was the lack of air conditioning in the apartment. Riding the subway, especially after work, was like living in a sub-tropical climate. By the time I got to the apartment I was a sweaty mess. The only option was to spend nights walking around the city (just as Mom said not to do). But I was never alone, so I felt safe.

One day after work, as I was dragging my sweaty body through the apartment lobby, I saw two guys getting out of the elevator; one tall and pale the other shorter and dark. Had the pale one been alone, I wouldn't have given him a second look. The other one was a different story. He was dark skinned with blue/black shiny hair that hung down around his head like a mop. His eyes were also jet black. When he saw me he smiled, exposing two rows of perfect white teeth. He took my breath away. Since he totally fit Sally's description, I figured he was Jason and the other one was Allen.

I debated saying something to them but decided to let things happen. If they really wanted to see Sally, they would be back. I got into the elevator and rode up to the 8th floor. I barely had time to shower and change into jeans and a tee shirt when I heard Sally coming through the door, laughing and talking loudly.

"Company's here," she yelled as she came toward me—the two guys behind her.

"I found these two wandering around Broadway; should we keep them?" she said.

"I don't know, "I replied. "Have they had their shots?"

That got a laugh and allowed me to adjust myself. Jason's eyes were shooting sparks at me. He was so appealing it was hard not to stare at him. Yet he smiled sheepishly, as if apologizing for something.

We all headed toward the living room and Sally whispered in my ear:

"What do you think of the Indian?" I smiled and nodded approvingly, yet I felt strangely uncomfortable with these visitors, especially Jason. He had a powerful effect on me and that was scary. I feared it would impact my resolve to stay clear of danger.

Soon Bob Dylan's "Subterranean Home Sick Blues" was blasting from the record player in the living room and Jason began to move around the floor, in perfect rhythm to the beat. His shirt, unbuttoned almost to his waist, revealed a dark hairless chest. His pants were skin tight, exhibiting a small waist and narrow hips. He wore a beaded necklace and several rings. The clothes and accessories were perfect for this man/child. When he saw me staring at him, he accentuated his moves as if inviting me to join him. I decided to escape to the kitchen, pretending I needed a drink. Even Dominic had never affected me this way. What was going on???

As I reached into the refrigerator for a coke I felt a hand on my shoulder. I jerked up and found myself staring into his coal-colored eyes.

"Got any wine in there?" His speech was slightly blurred, heavy with accent but I couldn't pin point the origin. I wasn't sure English was his native language.

I handed him the only beer in the fridge but he declined. By this time, I was almost shaking and he could see it. I told him there was a liquor store near the apartment and he suggested we go together.

At the liquor store, he selected a bottle of cheap Thunderbird wine and handed the clerk some crumpled bills from his back pocket. I wondered if these were the last of his funds. We passed a fruit and vegetable stand on the way home and he grabbed a couple of peaches, handing me one and biting into the other. When I reproached him for stealing, he innocently said to me:

"Well, sure, but how else am I supposed to feed myself? How do you do it?"

When I told him I had a job, he burst out laughing and congratulated himself for "having found a working girl". What did he mean by that?

Once we got inside the elevator of our building he leaned against the wall and stared at me with that bewitching grin. He puckered his lips and kept nodding at me; I was totally helpless and very glad when we got to our floor.

I smelled marijuana when we opened the apartment door and I heard company in the living room. Sally came toward Jason and grabbed him for a dance. I welcomed the separation. He simply had too much impact on me. He spelled trouble and for once, I didn't want any. I sat next to Allen and tried to find out where he was from.

"Never mind about me … there's nothing to say about a dead man," he told me.

I found this particularly strange and asked for an explanation. Allen said his epitaph should say that he and Woodie Guthrie had something in common.

"Woodie and I will both die of the same hereditary disease, which is in our blood. I won't live another year."

After some prodding, he told me he had Huntington's disease, a progressive brain disorder caused by a defective gene. I believed him and immediately felt sorry for him. At no time did I think he could be pulling my leg.

In an effort to stop this gloomy subject, I changed the subject to food—everyone was hungry and all we had in the house was a bag of potato chips, some dill pickles and a large chunk of cheddar cheese. Fortunately Sally had brought a large loaf of bread from Party Cake so we had enough to satisfy our marijuana cravings.

While we were getting stoned Sally and Jason had become wrapped around each other on the rug in the living room. They were oblivious to the rest of us and it looked like they were going to eat each other's mouths. Her denim skirt was up around her waist and he was trying to remove her panties. In a few minutes, thank goodness, they got off the floor and went into her room.

I decided to call it a night and headed toward my room. Allen asked if I wanted company but I respectfully declined, telling him I had to be at work early.

The next day was hell. I was extremely sleep deprived and found it hard to concentrate on my work. My supervisor Mandy noticed I was dragging and suggested I take a nap during my lunch hour. She told me to go to the TIME medical office on the 21st floor where they had cots. This turned out to be a brilliant idea, which I often relied on that summer.

When I got home from work, I heard James Brown singing before I opened the apartment door. When I got in Jason was dancing in the living room, in perfect rhythm; singing along with the lyrics. He saw me but kept right on with his sensual dancing. I escaped to my room to change.

When I got to the living room, Allen was sound asleep on the couch and Jason was straddling the open window and playing a harmonica. I asked where Sally was and Jason said she was out buying food. A few minutes later she came in with grocery bags and told me Brian was coming over, along with some other friends of hers.

A short time later, Brian arrived and I could tell by his facial expressions that he wasn't thrilled about our new friends but he accepted the joint being passed around. Then he got into a debate with Allen about the quality of the grass Allen had scored in the village. I could see this night was not going to end well. Brian took me by the hand and led me to my room.

"Who are these guys and when are they leaving?" Brian asked in an exasperated tone.

"They're friends of a friend and they just got here yesterday,"

"Yes, but when are they leaving?"

Now I was pissed and told him it was none of his business.

"Ok, you're right. But those guys are bad news. Can't you see that?"

Now I was super pissed: "What the hell are you talking about? They're just passing through; they're not living here!"

Brian said he was getting bad vibes from those guys and I should tell them to leave now. Then he tried to get me to go for a walk but I told him it was too damn hot and I walked back to the living room. Soon the front door opened and I heard it slammed shut.

The living room was now dark, the only light coming from several candles. Most of Sally's friends were sitting on the floor rolling joints. We smoked, ate and drank for the next several hours. Occasionally, Jason enticed one of the girls to dance with him or he sat on the window ledge playing his harmonica.

Desperately craving sleep, I slipped away to my room and started to undress. I was about to get into bed when the door opened slowly and I heard the harmonica. I turned around while shielding my naked breasts and Jason came in and closed the door.

"I thought you'd like some company tonight since your friend took off," he said with that arrogant grin of his.

He came toward me; my knees started to buckle. His hands went around my neck and his mouth came down hard on mine. As he kissed me, he led me to the bed and pushed me down on it. There was no struggle on my part. I had rehearsed this scene already.

He stopped kissing me, reached for the light on the night table and turned it off. Now the room was dark, except for the dim light coming from street lamps. He turned his body away from me and started undressing. He did it in a shy way, and it struck me as peculiar that he was so modest. When he was naked, he slowly twisted his body around and sat on the bed - careful to hide his penis. I was totally mystified that he appeared so vulnerable.

He kissed me again but kept his eyes half open, as if on the lookout for the unexpected. His motions were calculated and perfect, but they also reminded me of a wounded animal.

When he gently pushed into me, I briefly thought of the few times Dominic and I had made love. This was totally different yet very satisfying, but Jason seemed driven to something he knew he could not have. I asked him what was wrong. Was it me?

"It's not you. Don't worry," he said, kissing me. "It's my hang up. It's OK." He rolled off me and was quiet for a minute then he added "You're OK; real fine. You make it better for me; better than it's been for a long time."

CHAPTER 20

BE SURE TO WEAR SOME FLOWERS IN YOUR HAIR

CATHERINE

That first night with Jason led to many more similar ones and slowly I learned more about him. Although he claimed to be in his 20s, I never found out how old he was and I doubted his real name was Jason; he said he was a full-blooded American Indian. When I asked where he was born or where his family lived, he refused to talk about that and said he had been on his own for years. He claimed he dropped out of school when he was just 16 and that the only job he ever had was washing dishes. Eventually I learned why he had problems with sex. He confided he had sold his body to men, and that he often had been physically abused by these partners. This sad story awakened the mother in me and I decided he needed to be loved, as if he were my child. There were no more discussions about when he had to leave, other than when I had to go back to school.

When I looked back on that summer in the city, I realized Brian was the only sensible person I met. Before Sally and I fully realized what was happening, friends of Jason's and Allen's started showing up and staying. Soon we had more than a dozen kids living in that apartment; most of them street urchins who had nowhere else to go.

Maybe it was because I had, once again, become totally infatuated with a guy—one who mystified me but needed to be loved. Or maybe it was the "thrill" of living on the edge; far from what is normal and acceptable. Then there was Dominic and my need to keep him out of my life. Maybe I had to live this kind of life to really forget him. Naturally, my parents would have been horrified if they knew what was going on in the city. Obviously, I had not yet shed my need to rebel.

Yet no matter how much partying I did at night, I never missed a day of work at TIME but I was grateful for those cots on the 21st floor. Mandy noticed a change in me but since it never affected my work output she decided not to play mother and caution me about my choices.

Of all the kids who ended up passing through our apartment that summer, the two I remember most in addition to Jason and Allen were Julie and Tex. Together they didn't weigh 200 pounds and both dressed totally in black, highlighted by their paleness. They said they were Hell's Angels but that was most likely part of their shtick. Whoever they really were, they had a very unhealthy lifestyle—relying on little food and a lot of drugs. Tex also talked faster than anyone I knew, and most of what he said made little sense. Julie seemed like a terrified waif but she did help out with the cooking. Tex mostly kept the apartment supplied with drugs.

One night Julie overdosed. Tex swore he had not given her heroin but no one knew what she had taken. Before we could even call 911, we had to clear the apartment of drugs and people. By the time the emergency team arrived, Julie had awakened and thrown up all over the couch. She was taken to a hospital for observation and Tex went with her. I was left to clean up the couch and think about what could have happened if she had died. I finally had to admit I was living a dangerous lifestyle. After a brief hospital stay Julie recovered from the overdose and she and Tex decided to get on the road again.

A few days after this, Sally's father passed away unexpectedly and we went back to Middletown for the funeral. The shock of his death, coupled with having to make snap decisions, prevented us from doing the right thing—clearing out the apartment. We actually left Jason and Allen in charge! What were we thinking? Sally stayed for a week to help comfort her mother but I went back after two days because of my work.

When I walked into the apartment, the odor took my breath away. The stench of bodies, garbage and drugs was overwhelming and the apartment was trashed even more. There wasn't a piece of floor without a human or an article of clothing. My first reaction was to open the living room windows. Then I kicked everyone out, and told them they were no longer welcomed— except Jason and Allen of course.

By then I had just two weeks left at TIME and I was determined to meet all my project deadlines. Having that summer internship would look good on my resume and I needed a recommendation from Mandy. If TIME re-hired me after graduation, I could live in Manhattan again, and that was important to me.

When Sally returned from Middletown she had a bit of unwelcomed news for me.

"I ran into Dominic in town and he asked about you since he'd heard we were sharing an apartment in Manhattan," she said. "I'm sorry but he wanted to know where it was and I felt weird not telling him. So I'm afraid he might just show up!"

She was right. A couple of days later I found him in the living room when I got home from work; pacing like a mad man, his eyes dark with anger. No one else was in the apartment.

"Dominic, how did you get in?" I asked, not knowing what else to say although we hadn't talked or seen each other in over a year.

"That's all you can say to me after all this time? One of the freaks let me in," he answered. "What the hell is going on here, anyway? Who are these people you're living with? I thought it was just you and Sally?"

"They are friends of Sally's and they're just visiting," I blurted out, not able to come up with anything better. "You know this isn't just my apartment and she has the right to have her friends over."

He sat down on the couch and took a cigarette from the pack in his pocket. His hand was shaking so much he broke the cigarette and then threw it against the wall. He looked at me as if that was my fault.

"Why didn't you call to let me know you were in town?" I asked.

"I didn't think I had to. I thought you would be happy to see me. I wanted to surprise you but I'm the one who got the surprise!" he added, looking at me with dagger eyes.

"How long are you planning to stay?" I asked, hoping the answer was a very short while, even though not so long ago I would have hoped he would stay forever.

At that moment, Sally, Jason and Allen came into the apartment and it occurred to me they might have left to give me privacy when I came home and found Dominic. I immediately sensed a foreboding; and wished I could snap my fingers and make this day disappear.

The rest of the night went downhill rapidly. Jason and Allen started rolling joints and some of Sally's school friends showed up. Dominic started getting high and decided to vent his anger against me by hitting on one of Sally's friends, who promptly told him to get lost. He ignored me for the rest of the night, except to glare at me whenever he caught my eye.

Jason ended up totally wasted on Thunderbird wine and falling down in a drunken stupor. He was so out of it several of us put him in the shower with all of his clothes and turned on the cold water to revive him. In his delirious state he kept saying to me:

"Why didn't you tell me you had an old man?" He looked and acted like a wounded animal. I wondered what Dominic had told him before I had gotten home. I doubt Dominic had admitted the two of us hadn't been in contact for over a year.

In the end Dominic, who obviously had not smoked a lot of dope before, crashed on my bed; leaving me the floor to sleep on. In the morning, he stepped over me but I pretended to be asleep. He grabbed his duffel bag and left without saying goodbye. When I drank enough coffee to wake up, it occurred to me that I was no longer in love with him. After we had shared an intense, at times unhealthy attraction, and had seriously considered marriage just a few years ago, now there was nothing left—no sorrow, no pity and no tears. Our relationship officially ended in that apartment as if it had never started. I really didn't care if I ever saw him or heard from him again. But the impact of our relationship never ended for me. It would be my forever cross to bear.

For the rest of our time together, Sally and I kept reminding Jason and Allen we had to vacate the apartment soon. They finally told us they would hitch hike to California the day we left. Jason started pressuring me to come with him.

"We're headed to Haight Ashbury because that's where all the action is," he said. "You've got to come with me. I need you." And he was relentless.

After a few days of his constant pleadings, I actually began to consider going with him. Maybe it was because I had been living an alternative life most of that summer and my brain had been compromised. Or maybe I just didn't want to let him go because I didn't think he would survive on the streets. Or maybe, just maybe, I wanted to save him as atonement for the babies I had sacrificed. Whatever the motivation, I actually had serious thoughts about walking away from my life and thumbing my way to the west coast with him. I even had dreams of what it might look like—how we would make it across the country and what we would do once we got to San Francisco. I had seen this summer how these street kids had become expert at "pan handling"; begging for money. I knew that's how they got money to eat. The only way I gave any thought to going with Jason was that I consciously left my parents out of the equation. I never thought about how I could explain I was walking away from my last year of college to cross the country with a street child. I never gave any thought to how much this would break their hearts. I just knew I didn't want to give him up.

On our last day in the apartment I still hadn't told Jason what I had decided to do. Since I had packed all my things, he certainly could have assumed I was going with him. When it was time for all of us to leave, I went down to the lobby with him and sat on the bench near the front door. His eyes were pleading, and he was telling me that I was the first person who had ever cared about him. He said he was nothing without me. As he talked, my mind was racing and I thought about the last three years and how I was determined to get that degree and not disappoint my parents. That's what allowed me to make the right decision in that split second —to forego an adventure, albeit a very dangerous one, and stay on the right path to make my parents proud. I certainly owed them that, and I owed myself a better future.

That's when I realized Mom and Dad had been good parents. In spite of my mistakes they had given me the freedom to pursue a goal while instilling in me the necessary values to keep going in the right direction. I could not break their hearts again by leaving my education behind to hitchhike to California. I grabbed Jason's face and gave him a long kiss.

"I will remember you always but I cannot come with you. You have to accept that," I said. "Please take care of yourself."

I walked away quickly so he would not see my tears and I

took the elevator to the eighth floor. The summer was over and once more I had survived against the odds.

Many years after this summer, while packing for yet another move, I was going through my music LPs and noticed something stuck in the cover of the Sergeant Pepper's Lonely Hearts Club Band album. I pulled out the pieces and saw it was a large photo of the Beatles but it had something written on the back side. In order to read it, I had to tape the pieces back together. In a very childish handwriting, it read:

"I love you Cat. Never forget me please. Although you may have had some feelings for me, I am still lonely but will never forget you. I'm nothing anyway so why bother? I'm just a street kid and you're a college girl. But whatever you showed me, I love you and don't you forget it. Some day you'll meet someone who will really love you and want you for the rest of your life." It was signed Love, Jason

CHAPTER 21

LOVE AND MARRIAGE

CATHERINE

Marie-Anne and I went back to Skidmore for our senior year in the fall of 1967. She never knew what had taken place in Manhattan but when I ended up in the college's infirmary soon after we got to campus, she was concerned. The attending medical staff said I was suffering from exhaustion and mostly just needed rest. I told Marie-Anne there was nothing to worry about and asked her not to tell our parents I was in the infirmary. This was the first time I asked her to cover for me and she agreed.

The fall semester ended without any other issues. When we went home for Christmas Marie-Anne started spending time with a guy we knew from our high school days. Rob was Korean and had been very popular in high school but our parents didn't consider him good enough for their daughter. We were told it had nothing to do with his being Asian but rather it was because he had not finished college and didn't intend to.

Soon after our graduation in June 1968, Marie-Anne and I moved into an apartment in Manhattan on East 80th street. She was working at the Rockefeller Institute and TIME had hired me back in the market research department.

That Fall Sally called and said she wanted to fix me up with someone who was rooming with the guy she was dating. They were both seniors at Columbia and when she had told Richard about me he said he wanted to meet me. We had that blind date, where I learned how to play pool and appreciate good Scotch, and from that point on Richard and I were inseparable. Either I would spend the night at his apartment on the upper West side or he would come to my place on the East side. Marie-Anne never minded as she often had our apartment to herself with Rob. Naturally, I immediately told Mom and Dad I was dating an Ivy Leaguer. I knew that would impress them.

At Thanksgiving, Marie-Anne announced, to our parents' chagrin, that she intended to marry Rob whether they approved or not. How did our mother react to this? She told Marie-Anne to "GET OUT!" and took a chapter from Jewish culture by throwing Marie-Anne's mattress out on the street. No wonder Dad often said: "Your mother is unique!"

The Jews are far more practical. When a member of the family goes "against the grain" they simply tear a piece of their suit jacket. Our father reacted quite differently from Mom. He summoned Rob to the house and told him he was a big Zero and would never amount to anything— so he should just leave Marie-Anne alone.

The love birds were not discouraged by our parents' reactions and continued spending time together. I was thrilled my sister was finally rebelling and, naturally, I was totally on her side.

In January 1969, Marie-Anne and Rob were married by a Justice of the Peace with Richard and me serving as witnesses. The four of us went to a Steak and Ale in Manhattan to celebrate and that was that. They moved into a small apartment in Nyack and she got a new job as a technician at a Tarrytown Lab; Rob was selling furniture in Nyack, fine-tuning his natural gift as a salesman. Mom and Dad pretended none of this was going on. Clearly they were in denial their perfect daughter had gone against them.

Since I was spending every night with Richard and had lost my roommate, I moved out of our East side apartment and into his. He graduated from Columbia in June but I was not invited to his graduation since he had not yet told his parents about me. That bit of information should have been a heads up since we had been living together for months but I was in love so I pushed it aside. Besides, he now held a degree from an Ivy League college so my parents were excited. Soon after that I brought him home so they could meet him. They were very pleased to see I had finally picked someone they deemed acceptable, especially since Marie-Anne was now the one with the unacceptable mate.

Richard had been dabbling in photography during his last year at Columbia and prior to meeting me had decided to pursue a graduate degree in film. That all changed when we got together and he chose instead to stay in Manhattan and get into the film business there. He landed a job with a small commercial film company, working as a grip on food commercials. One of the highlights of his job was the night his company was invited to a screening of Mel Brooks' "The Twelve Chairs" and we were there along with Mel and his wife Anne Bancroft. Another highlight was the day I was "on the set" of a movie they were filming in the Bronx about drug addiction.

In the meantime, I had left TIME when I was hired by one of its advertising clients— Hystron Fibers—still in the secretarial pool, but given a salary bump. Richard and I had been together for more than one year and Mom said he should make his intentions known prior to coming to her house again. When I shared that information with Richard, he agreed it was time to tell his parents about me. His mother did not react well when she learned her only child intended on getting married. She blamed Sally for introducing us and told her I had "pulled the rug out from under Richard" because I was forcing him to marry me.

When I finally met his parents, only two months before we got married, I understood why he had waited so long to tell his mother about us. She absolutely dotted on him and saw me as a threat. His father was charming and welcomed me with a very big smile that spelled relief.

We were married on June 6, 1970, D Day in Europe, with a small gathering of family and friends at Mom and Dad's house. They gave us a choice between a big wedding or a small affair, with additional money for a honeymoon in France and Italy. We chose the latter. A Lutheran minister affiliated with Columbia University delivered the vows. I wore a gypsy skirt and see-through blouse, minus bra. Mom made sure my long dark hair covered my nipples. Richard wore dark pants and a Mexican wedding shirt. He too had long hair. It was very much a hippy kind of wedding. After lunch we threw Frisbees around the back yard and drank a lot of French champagne. Marie-Anne was there alone as Rob was still persona non-grata in our family.

Shortly before the wedding we had moved into a newly-updated apartment in a row house on 95th Street between Columbus and Amsterdam Avenues. It was just one floor, long and narrow, with a closet-sized kitchen and a balcony beyond the bedroom. It was tiny but had all new paint and refinished floors and the monthly rent was only $90. We loved it.

The following summer we flew to France and stayed with Charles and Zaza in their new apartment in Cannes. They had sold both of their houses as well as the ceramic business and were now spending days playing bridge with other retired folks. Through connections, Charles got tickets for us to the Cannes Film Festival where we saw one of the first movies Al Paccino ever made—"The Panic in Needle Park". We had several dinners with Mamie Charlotte and Roger and then took the train to Florence, then Venice and finally Portofino. Since we were in Venice for our one year anniversary, Dad insisted on us staying at the Hotel Danieli, a five star establishment, and eating in their fine dining room—where we were the only couple in our twenties and earned lots of stares from the other guests.

Back home the honeymoon ended abruptly when Richard lost his job. Faced with not being able to find another job in the film industry quickly, he resorted to driving a cab in New York City. That gave him a lot of time to think about his future and he decided to go to graduate school after all for a degree in developmental psychology. He applied to several schools and got into a program at Rutgers University. So we left Manhattan and moved to New Jersey in the spring of 1972. I got a job in the Rutgers publications office, proofreading their countless catalogues— a very boring job, but it helped pay the bills.

Initially, we rented an old farmhouse west of Flemington, New Jersey. It was in the middle of nowhere and a far cry from the streets of Manhattan but we planted a vegetable garden, got some chickens and a Beagle puppy, a fine addition to our several cats. We became instant farmers.

"What possessed you to get a Beagle?" asked Dad who thought only Dachshunds were proper dogs. "Beagles are only bred to bark while running!"

The farmhouse started losing its charm when winter came and the furnace never quite functioned properly. Then the chickens all died and the Beagle ran away one day; resulting in an hours' search in the country—fortunately successful. Then there was the LONG commute to New Brunswick for Richard's classes and my job. We started exploring other living situations.

Through a friend we learned of a position as a tenant farmer in Cokesbury, New Jersey, which was much closer to New Brunswick. We would get a free house in return for 15 hours of work each week, taking care of Sardinian donkeys—the kind wealthy people buy for their kids because they are small enough to keep in a fenced yard. We applied for the job and got it. Unfortunately we were not able to see the inside of the house we would occupy as the current tenant farmer was still there.

We were not told the current farmer had lived there 30 years and the farm owners had not seen the inside of the house all those years. When we were finally admitted inside, we knew we had made a mistake but it was too late to back out since the Flemington farmhouse had already been rented. After spending entire days sanding floors, painting and cleaning we moved into the house mid April 1973. Richard's 15 hours of work consisted of feeding the donkeys and mucking their stalls. We had told the farm's owners he was a graduate student with teaching responsibilities and I worked full-time at Rutgers.

On May 3 we went out to dinner to celebrate my birthday. The next day, the farm's owner called us in and chastised us for leaving without telling him. That's when we learned a lot more was expected of us beyond those 15 hours a week. So although we had spent hours and many dollars rehabbing the old farmhouse, we moved out of there quickly and luckily found a rental—a beautiful Victorian home in Annandale, New Jersey, just up the highway from the donkey farm.

In spite of these setbacks at the beginning of the seventies there was a happy milestone in our family. Early in 1972 we learned Marie-Anne and Rob were expecting their first child in November. By then Marie-Anne was allowed back in the Middletown home to visit but her husband was still not welcomed. When Marie-Anne announced she was pregnant, unfortunately doing so on April Fools' Day, not everyone was excited.

"Just what we need – more rice in the world," exclaimed Mom, never one to miss an opportunity for sarcasm.

When Courtney Elizabeth joined our family on November 3, 1972, she was placed in the nursery next to the only other Asian child whose mother was Japanese. When Marie-Anne took Mom down to the nursery she pointed to the two babies and said:

"OK, pick which one she is." She had finally learned to deal with Mom.

Courtney was a beautiful child and as the first grandchild in the family she has continued to hold a place of honor. When Mamie Charlotte wanted to come see her she told Mom she would only come if Marie-Anne and Rob were both welcomed in the house. So Courtney was the catalyst for finally ending the family detente.

She was also the motivation for more grandchildren. During every phone conversation I had with Marie-Anne, I learned of another example of the wonders of having a baby. I started making noises about wanting my own child. When Courtney was six months old, I borrowed her for the weekend to see what it was like to be a Mom. Little did I know she was an ideal infant; she slept, she ate, and she smiled. Taking care of her was a piece of cake. Of course I could do this. I started working on Richard to agree with me.

What could possibly go wrong?

CHAPTER 22

ONE OF THE LUCKY ONES

CATHERINE

It took nearly a year but I finally convinced Richard we should start a family. I promised to continue working until I delivered and to go back to work right after the baby was born. We could not make it on his teaching assistant salary alone but I so badly wanted a child, I was willing to move earth to make it happen.

In 1973, just after my 26th birthday, I learned I was pregnant. I was ecstatic as I had feared the abortions might have made me infertile. I really wanted a child.

By then Richard was a psychology doctoral candidate, and still had a couple of years of graduate school ahead of him. Although I knew very few women then who went back to work after having a baby, I believed I could do it. Since I was young, healthy and excelled at multi-tasking I intended to work until my due date and then use my two weeks' vacation to recuperate after the baby was born. I figured all we would need to do is find reliable child care.

While Mom warned I might be tackling more than I could handle, I told her about one of Richard's professors who had twins the previous year and went back to work when they were just a month old. I failed to mention her mother moved in with her for the first year.

For my prenatal care and delivery, we chose Dr. Gerald Barrard an OB/GYN at the Hunterdon Medical Center in Flemington, New Jersey because we had heard he encouraged fathers to be in the delivery room. He also promoted Ferris Urbanowski's Lamaze classes for parents who wanted medication-free deliveries. Ferris had moved to Bucks County Pennsylvania from California after she starred in the film *The Story of Eric*, which follows a couple through pregnancy Lamaze classes and the birth of their first child.

We started attending her Lamaze classes in December 1973 and ended up being one of the couples featured in her book *Lamaze for New Parents,* published in 1975. Because we had agreed to be featured in the book, Ferris gave each mother a free Yoga class once the baby was born.

On January 25, 1974 Richard and I—with Dr. Barrard assisting of course—delivered our daughter Zoë using pure Lamaze; no drugs of any kind. I will always remember being in the labor room for hours doing my Lamaze breathing faithfully. The pains were getting stronger and more frequent but I would not accept any drugs. Suddenly I saw bright lights on in the delivery room and I knew it was for me since I was the only one in labor. Zoë arrived with little effort and she was beyond perfect. The nurse put her on my stomach and I felt tremendous relief— she was here, she was healthy and I was finally a Mom! I was elated beyond description and became so agitated on the delivery table, the nurse took Zoë away to make sure I wouldn't drop her.

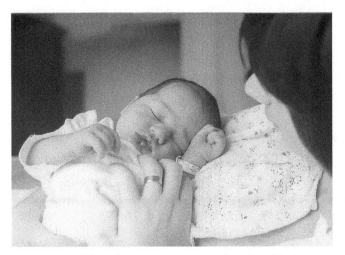

Zoë and Catherine, minutes after her birth

Since I had been such a cooperative Lamaze patient, Dr. Barrard encouraged me to walk to my room right after the delivery. I suppose he considered it a "victory walk." He was right. I had just won the best prize in the world. In fact, I don't believe my feet touched the floor; I was in another world of sheer joy. I couldn't stop talking about Zoë and how beautiful she was. I kept asking when she would be in my room so I could hold her again. Unfortunately she was slightly jaundiced so she had to stay in the nursery under Bilirubin lights; depriving me of the joy of immediate bonding. My father in law came to visit the next day and he was the first to notice I was far more hyper than usual.

"It's totally normal to be on a natural high after giving birth" Richard told his father, as if he'd experienced birth himself.

When we got home with Zoë, our friends Ed and Anne came to visit. Ed was also a psychology graduate student and he too noticed something was not right.

"I've never seen her this wild before. Aren't you worried?" he asked Richard.

Again Richard said I was just thrilled to be a mom. He didn't tell Ed about the abortions because he knew I wanted to keep that a secret. Richard thought I was hyper from being thrilled to be a mother this time.

When Zoë was just one week old, I asked Mom if she wanted to go to the Yoga class with me. She thought it was way too early to be out with an infant but she agreed to come. She drove from Middletown to Annandale and together with Zoë in the car seat we drove to New Hope, PA for the class. I talked a lot and very fast during that ride and I wondered why Mom was looking at me so strangely.

"Are you alright?" Mom asked me several times. "Why are you talking so fast?"

"I'm just happy, that's all," I kept saying. And I was. I had been blessed with a beautiful and healthy daughter and I couldn't believe I had been so lucky. I knew I didn't deserve it.

The Yoga class was held in a beautiful modern house in New Hope, Pennsylvania, high up on a hill and with large windows that looked out on the countryside. Several other new Moms from our class were there and it was great to see them with their babies. I wondered why they also looked at me strangely.

Several days after the class I had a total breakdown. I don't recall what specifically led to this but I was severely sleep deprived by then. I locked myself in the bathroom and screamed that I was going to kill myself. Richard had to use an ax to tear down the door to get to me. Our friends Ed and Anne came right away and told Richard he should take me to the hospital.

While Anne stayed with Zoë, Richard and Ed drove me to the Hunterdon Medical Center. Ed had to hold me in his arms the whole ride to keep me from opening the car door to escape.

When we arrived, we were led to a reception area. The only thing I remember from that night is seeing a copy of TIME Magazine in the waiting room with Bob Dylan on the cover, but Dylan's face morphed to Dominic's and I started screaming. Several people in white coats appeared and led me to an observation room, where I was strapped down in a bed and given a shot. Then everything went dark.

Richard learned the diagnosis—acute post partum depression. The medical center staff gave him the name of a psychiatrist and urged him to make an appointment immediately. Rather than trust my care to a stranger, he chose to rely on a couple of his professors who doubled as therapists. One of them was the professor who had twins and soon I accused Richard of having an affair with her. Paranoia was very much part of this psychosis.

Then I started seeing one of Richard's male professors but since there was no progress he recommended a psychiatrist affiliated with Rutgers University. His name was Dr. Steven Targum but I will forever think of him as my savior.

For much of 1974 I was essentially checked out, mostly because of depression and medication. Major events happened but I don't recall any of them. I had to quit my job since I was not functioning. Richard had to escort me on the unemployment line so I could collect benefits (my employer was kind enough to say I had been let go).

Since we could no longer afford to pay rent, we had to move into my in laws' house in another part of the state. I don't recall any of this. As to who was taking care of Zoë? Fortunately, we initially had friends, neighbors and family members who took turns so that Richard could continue his studies. Eventually Richard found a full time sitter who was appropriately named Mrs. Cope.

I also have no memory of spending a weekend with my in-laws at Lake George when I had another meltdown and had to be hospitalized. I was later told I became hysterical when we tried to go for a boat ride and I thought I would drown. Finally, I don't recall trying to electrocute myself, but I was told I did that as well.

That's when Dr. Targum told Richard that therapy and medication would not improve my condition. He urged him to have me committed to Carrier Clinic in Belle Mead, New Jersey for electroconvulsive treatments (ECT).

Richard spent hours in the library researching this very controversial technique and told my doctor he was completely against it. When Dr. Targum failed to convince him that it was either ECT or long-term hospitalization, the good doctor called my parents and asked if they would go to court with him to have Richard re-consider. They were willing to do whatever it took to fix me, they said.

Richard relented and I was admitted to Carrier Clinic in early September.

I had lost more than half the year and I still did not know I had a child. When Mom came to visit me she brought Zoë, and I chastised her for having another child at her age. Every night at Carrier I would put all of my clothes in the garbage. Every morning the nurse would retrieve them for me. I didn't know who or where I was. I was barely functioning as a toddler.

During the electroconvulsive treatments medical staff would strap me down on a bed and place rubber in my mouth to keep me from biting my tongue. Once a sedative was administered so I would not feel anything, the shocks were administered. I do not recall any of the first seven treatments. I only remember the eighth one.

When I first started seeing Dr. Targum he had asked my parents to describe my personality prior to Zoë's birth since he only knew me as severely depressed. They told him I was a happy, productive person with lots of opinions I was not shy to express. One day, after the treatment was over, the nurse gave me the customary glass of orange juice because the sugar was somehow helpful after the procedure. This particular glass of juice had gone bad so I spat it out and shouted

"This tastes like shit!"

I saw Dr. Targum smile and then he ran out of the room. Later my mother told me he had called her and said "She's back!"

Slowly I remembered who I was and I began asking where I was and why. Then one day Richard brought Zoë. When I saw her I broke down and sobbed. I finally remembered she was my child and realized I had missed the first nine months of her life.

When I was released from Carrier after nearly ten weeks, I had to re-learn many life skills since the treatments had severely affected my memory. I had forgotten how to drive, how to take care of myself and a house and how to cook. During my first outing to a grocery store, Richard had to identify the fruits and vegetables I liked.

I also had to learn how to care for Zoë, with whom I had yet to bond.

I will never know for certain why I had a breakdown. But I am fairly sure the abortions played a major role. I had never allowed myself to grieve for those babies nor did I deal with the shame of taking two lives. All of this came crashing down on me the moment Zoë was laid in my arms; that's when I realized how wrong those decisions had been. I cannot forgive myself for making the wrong choices. I know how much that breakdown cost me—I missed most of Zoë's first year and that has been my life's regret. While the shock treatments saved me from potential life-long hospitalization, they also robbed me of crucial memories, some of which I still have not recovered.

Since I'd had such a severe case of depression, Dr. Targum prescribed the mood stabilizer Lithium and told me I should stay on it for the rest of my life. Because it was contraindicated for pregnancy, I was told I would not be able to have another child.

Since I could not go back to work yet, Richard left graduate school and accepted a teaching position at Marywood College in Scranton, Pennsylvania. We moved again to a hole in the wall little town called South Canaan where we rented a beat up old house for a mere $100 a month. It was down the street from the Lockwood Store, where everybody knew your name.

One day when a bout of nausea indicated the Lithium dose

might be too high my doctor told me to stay off of it for a couple of days; I saw this as an opportunity to see if I really needed it. When I did not experience any depression or manic behavior I stopped taking Lithium by spring 1975.

I was one of the lucky ones. This time I had escaped the wrath of unintended consequences.

Two years later when Zoë's brother Caleb was born I did not have another episode. I didn't even have the baby blues.

CHAPTER 23

CALIFORNIA DREAMIN'

GABE

By the mid seventies, we had been in America nearly twenty years. I had continued earning accolades for my creations at Polak's Frutal Works; raises and bonuses kept increasing. When I spoke with perfumers who worked for other companies, and by then there were quite of few of them in the States, I learned I had a great deal; a ten minute drive to work, a very small mortgage on a nice house and a small American town without traffic. After what we had been through in France we considered ourselves very lucky things had turned out so well.

Of course not everything went smoothly. First Claudine had cancer but now that it had been fifteen years since her surgery we could stop worrying it might come back. Then Catherine had gotten pregnant but fortunately we made her realize she was simply not ready to have a child. She had straightened out, graduated from college and even found an Ivy League graduate for a husband. Marie-Anne hadn't chosen as wisely—the first time she had ever gone against our wishes. She was old enough to choose her path and we hoped the best for her. She also gave us our first grandchild, and Courtney was a delight.

Just when we thought everything was great, Catherine had a

breakdown after her daughter Zoë was born in 1974. We don't know why this happened. No one in my family or Claudine's ever had that kind of breakdown. Thankfully, the shock treatments had worked and the medication she was taking seemed to keep her stabilized. We hoped she wouldn't rush back to work as that would put too much strain on her. Since Richard was now teaching at a Pennsylvania College there was less pressure for her to have a job. We also thought she should be home with her daughter.

Just as I assumed everything would continue on a positive note, Bernard Polak announced he had sold his company to Hercules, Inc., a major US conglomerate that was not in the perfume or flavors business. This concerned me because I did not want to work for a large company, especially one that hired chemists rather than perfumers. I feared this would really limit my creativity.

Before the sale was even finalized, I began thinking about our options. I was now 54 and I didn't want to work until I was too old to enjoy life. My father had died at 62 and I figured that's when I would die as well. The Polak salary plus our small mortgage payment allowed us to save quite a bit of money and invest it well. Perhaps it was time to consider another part of the country—one that would allow me to spend more time outside, and even have a sail boat.

I started dreaming about moving to California.

When Bernard Polak called me in for the end of year review, giving me high marks again and a very nice bonus, I informed him I would give him another six months but that was it. I told him we were moving to California. The job had stopped being fun and it was time for me to enjoy life.

CLAUDINE

It was a typical day, starting with coffee at Claire's in the morning. After lunch, when Gabe went back to work, I went to town for some Christmas shopping. As usual, Gabe came home at 5:10 sharp.

"I have a surprise for you," he said as he walked through the kitchen. I knew he was meeting with Bernard that day and most likely the surprise was another nice bonus. "How much did you get?" I asked him.

"I got a very nice bonus. But that's not all," he says. "I have resigned my position at Polak's" he announced with a large smile.

I thought I must have heard wrong. He quit his job? My facial expression telegraphed my surprise.

"You're joking, right?" I hoped.

"No. I'm dead serious. I told Bernard he'd have me another six months and that was it," he explained.

There had been many big decisions Gabe had made without consulting me—such as buying that Jaguar —but quitting his job when we still had two kids to put through college?

Then he hits me with this.

"I've been thinking about this ever since I learned they were selling the company to Hercules. I didn't think that would work for me and it hasn't. The job just isn't fun anymore and I don't have enough vacation time. I want to retire and travel, before I am too old to enjoy life," he added.

Then he hits me with this final bit of news: "We're moving to California."

That was that. He had made the decision and I had no vote. I would have to leave Claire and Michelle, a town and a home I loved and go live on the West Coast where I knew no one. I also would have to give up my volunteer job at Horton Hospital. I was stunned but I knew better than to question his decision.

We stayed in Middletown through June 1975 because Steve was graduating from the Millbrook School that month. He had been accepted at Skidmore, the first year they took in male students, but Gabe convinced him to come to the West coast with us so he could teach him the perfume business. He said Steve could always go to a college out there, while living at home. Steve also had no choice in this. Kim broke down and cried when she learned we would be moving. She was only 15 and had lots of friends in Middletown. Like the rest of us she didn't have a vote.

Steve's high school graduation, June 1975- first row, left to right: Marie-Anne, Kim holding her niece Courtney, Catherine, Claudine and Steve. Second row, left to right: Roger, Mamie Charlotte, Richard with Zoë on his shoulders, Gabe.

Gabe decided we would move to the Bay area, to be near water so he could have a sail boat. When the word spread throughout the industry that he was leaving Polak's, Clorox offered him a consulting contract which he accepted. In the spring we flew out to San Francisco and put a deposit down on a house in Menlo Park.

Our realtor told us the first $100K you pay for a house in California is just for the sunshine. The price goes up from there.

The house we found was nice but very expensive. Aside from that, the backyard was too small for a pool and we had all been very spoiled in Middletown because we had added one. Again, I wasn't asked for my opinion.

GABE

When the word got out that I was leaving Polak's in June, Clorox offered me a job. I told them I was not interested in a full time position but I would consider consulting work. I had learned from industry contacts that there was a lot of money in consulting. Clorox offered me a great deal – a two year contract making twice as much as I made at Polak's, and I could do much of the work from home. Since their corporate office was in the Bay area, I asked a Polak's salesperson who lived there where we should look for a house. He lived in Menlo Park and recommended that town and that's why I chose it.

I also decided we would drive out to California when we moved because I refused to put Oliver on a plane, and we had to drive two cars out there anyway. The Jaguar went on the truck and I drove Claudine's station wagon, with Oliver in her lap and the back of the car filled with personal items we didn't trust with movers. We had given Steve a car when he graduated from Millbrook so he could drive that and take Kim with him. She was not in the best of mood at the time, so far better for her to ride with Steve.

We would take the northern route, going west on 80 since that highway went practically coast to coast. To get to 80, we had to go through eastern Pennsylvania and that was fine because we wanted to stop in South Canaan to see Catherine and the baby. We were concerned about how she was dealing with her current situation.

Richard had gotten a teaching position at Marywood College in Scranton, Pennsylvania. Instead of living in town they had rented a very old house in a little town called South Canaan. It had a general store and a post office. That's it. It was so remote it's where Patty Hearst was hiding out in 1974 when she was on the lam with the Symbionese Liberation Army.

When we got to South Canaan, I was shocked to see the house they rented looked like it might tip over at any time. It was a small, two story depressed box of a house that had no redeeming value. I couldn't imagine how this environment would help Catherine's mental health.

Then Catherine announced she had a surprise for us.

"I'm going back to work as PR director for Marywood College," she told us. "We have found a baby sitter for Zoë. I start next week."

We were shocked. Zoë was only 17 months old and none of us thought this was a good idea. But it was obvious the decision was made so we could only hope it would not end badly. All we could do was wish her well and worry.

Catherine seemed to have recovered, but since none of us had ever known anyone who'd had a breakdown we were not in a position to challenge her decision to go back to work. We assumed they needed two incomes.

We were all outside after dinner, enjoying the nice weather, when all of a sudden I rocked myself backwards right out of the chair. I landed flat on my back still attached to the chair and everyone was laughing.

Fortunately, I landed on the lawn so I didn't hurt myself, but I couldn't help think back to the time I fell at Juliette-Antoinette and dislocated my shoulder. I wondered if this fall might be some kind of omen about our road trip or our life in California. I also feared it could be an omen about Catherine going back to work.

Fortunately nothing else happened during the drive and we got to see so much of the country we had never seen before. It's not possible to appreciate how spectacular this country is until you travel by car from coast to coast. We didn't drive more than seven hours each day so it took us more than a week to get to Menlo Park. Claudine was thrilled because she got to fulfill one of her dreams—to spend a night in Cheyenne, Wyoming.

Just as important, Catherine had no adverse effects when she started working again. In fact, she managed a successful career that took her to four other states; but that would come later.

CLAUDINE

The kids were very helpful when the moving van arrived in Menlo Park and soon we were all set up in our new home. Gabe took one of the bedrooms for his office and he found a carpenter who made him a home "organ" for his consulting work. He also started teaching Steve about the perfume business.

Some of our neighbors came over to welcome us to the neighborhood and from one of them I learned there was a new comers' club in town. Since we knew no one, I decided we should join. So that's what I did. I actually made a decision all by myself! Gabe said I was crazy to join a group of people we didn't know but he eventually agreed it was a good idea because we ended up with friends quickly.

A few months later one of the group's members asked me if I was interested in a part-time job in a high-end gift shop in town. Me! I told her the only job I had ever had was packing pottery for my relative's ceramic business. What could I possibly have to offer?

"But Claudine, your French background and the knowledge you have about china and crystal—that would be perfect at Julie's," she said.

Julie had opened the shop in 1972 and needed another sales

person. Without even telling Gabe, I went to see her; we hit it off right away and she hired me! She said my French accent would add a special touch. When I told Gabe I had a job he thought I was kidding.

"A job? Who will take care of the house and the kids? Who will make my lunch?" he asked.

I reminded him the kids could now take care of themselves and I intended to hire a cleaning lady since I would be making money. As to lunch, he would be on his own! He was stunned I had made these decisions without consulting him. I ended up working at Julie's for years, and she trusted me so much she left me in charge of the store when she went abroad to buy merchandise. Gabe finally had to admit he was proud of me!

In the end, the years we spent in California were some of the best of our lives. We never regained the same lifestyle we had in Golfe-Juan, but in my opinion we were happier. I finally stopped worrying so much.

GABE

It all came together quite well in California. Steve was a quick learner and absorbed the perfume business with keen interest. He enrolled in a community college, majored in business, and even had time for a part-time job. Once Kim got over her anger about being wrenched from her Middletown friends, she too acclimated to her new life and acquired lots of friends.

Claudine surprised me the most. She immediately got around the neighborhood and once again her French background and accent opened many doors for her. We had barely been there a couple of months when she announced she'd gotten herself a job! I was stunned. Without even asking for my opinion, she interviewed for a sales position at Julie's—a very high end gift shop in Menlo Park. She was such a quick learner she got a raise after just two months!

The California move was a stellar decision and the Clorox consulting gig worked out magnificently well. The very next year we moved to Atherton, CA into a bigger house on a couple of acres in the Lindenwood community; a high end neighborhood. Claudine was thrilled because we put in a pool and the schools were among the best in the Bay area—something Kim also appreciated.

Claudine often talks about our three "disasters"—the bankruptcy in 1954; her cancer in 1964; and Catherine's breakdown in 1974 and how it's bizarre they each occurred exactly ten years apart. Like our birds in France who all died right after the bankruptcy, she now considers all future years ending in "4" as potential disasters. When she goes down this path, she naturally wonders what will happen in 1984 (notwithstanding George Orwell's dystopian science fiction novel) and beyond that year. I keep telling her to stay focused on the present and how good things are for us right now.

Catherine asked me once what I had learned from our adventures. This is what I told her: I learned two things: one, give respect and consideration to any individual only in the same measure you get the same from that individual. Two, NEVER, NEVER, NEVER be impressed or influenced by MONEY! Money comes and goes. Only one's inner values count and remain. You have plenty of the right values, Catherine. Right on! I'm proud of you!!

ALAMO, CALIFORNIA JULY 2002

CATHERINE

We were together at Marie-Anne's house in Alamo. I was living in San Ramon, California. Both of us had divorced, re-married and had grown children. Kim, also divorced and re-married, and Steve were raising their families in New Jersey. We were celebrating my becoming a grandmother for the first time.

Dad had retired decades ago. After living in the Bay area, they moved to San Diego so he could have that sail boat again. When Marie-Anne moved to the Bay area in the late 80s, he and Mom left southern California and moved to Danville to be near her. They now had nine grandchildren and three great-grandchildren. All of us were doing well—in health, careers and financial stability.

Dad and I were together in the living room, sipping Chivas and talking about the state of things. In spite of Mom's premonitions, nothing bad happened in 1984 or 1994 and all the disasters we expected from the turn of the millennium didn't happen either. That naturally led me to comment on how fortunate we were.

"We are all blessed to be doing so well, even after setbacks and challenges. Don't you agree?"

I was not prepared for his answer.

"I don't know. I have often wondered what our lives would have been like had we stayed in France? I wonder if things would have been better."

I was shocked and could not understand why he still thought leaving France was a mistake.

"How much better could things have been in France, compared to our lives today?" I asked him.

His eyes clouded with sadness when he spoke again:

"It's something I will never know. Back in 1956 there were no other options and, frankly, I was mortified by the whole experience. How could I have been so naïve? We had an amazing life and I lost it all! I never considered the consequences of hiring the wrong person."

That's when I realized he had never forgiven himself for causing the events that led to leaving France. In spite of having made the hard decision to leave, then struggling to rebuild his reputation and finally making an impressive come-back—he still wondered "what if?"

Regrets never leave you, no matter how well you survive those unintended consequences. I too have unforgivable regrets. I am indeed one of the lucky ones—and I am thankful for many undeserved blessings that have come my way.

Raphel family celebrating Claudine's 85ᵗʰ and Gabe's 90ᵗʰ in North Barrington, Illinois. Seated: Claudine, Gabe and Catherine. Standing: Kim, Steve and Marie-Anne

ACKNOWLEDGEMENT

Like all other books, this was a work of love involving many people who encouraged me, refreshed my memory, provided feedback and created or enhanced photographs. These include:

Mom and Dad— who were brave beyond measure—and pleased to commit their stories to paper. I wish life's demands had not kept me from finishing this book earlier so they could have read it. Dad passed away in August 2010 and Mom in November 2019. Tragically, their youngest child Kim passed before Mom in 2016, after a brave seven year battle with breast cancer.

My sister and best friend Marie-Anne Reilly who read the book in manuscript form and confirmed it really all happened. Thank you LS for being there all my life and keeping me on the straight and narrow, much of the time.

My daughter Zoë Wetzel Byer, who read many chapters, provided wonderful feedback, and heaps of encouragement. Plus she made me a very lucky mom.

Rebecca W. Bass, photographer extraordinaire, who enhanced decades-old photographs while recuperating from surgery and shot my author's photo.

Low Country Writers Workshop in Beaufort, SC for their honest comments and suggestions for improvements.

Dr. Steven Targum saved me from a life of depression. This allowed me to be a Mom twice and have a productive life. I found him after 47 years and he remembered me as I was the only patient for whom he had recommended ECT; the only treatment option then. Today, there are many more choices for depression.

Finally—but most importantly—my husband David, who spent hours reading and re-reading chapters, provided invaluable feedback and was my strongest cheerleader. You are my rock and inspiration. Thank you for getting me toward this important goal.

ABOUT THE AUTHOR

Catherine Raphel Stewart spent more than four decades in public relations and marketing communications and has written short stories and a novella for her graduate degree, *Summer in the Life*. After her childhood in France, Stewart lived in six states. She is now retired and resides in Beaufort, South Carolina, with her husband, David, and their two dogs.